Alex, Cissy and *Paris* are trademarks of the Alexander Doll Company. *Barbie*® doll, *Audrey Hepburn* doll, and *Elizabeth Taylor* doll are the trademarks of Mattel, Inc. *Gene*® and *Madra* are trademarks of Mel Odom. *Tyler Wentworth* is a trademark of the Robert Tonner Doll Company. This book is an independent study by the authors. The research and publication of this book was not sponsored in any way by the manufacturers of the dolls used as examples or suppliers of the products used.

> *Overleaf, Mattel's Silkstone Barbie*® *doll in a lace covered buckram hat, designed exclusively by Timothy J. Alberts.*

Additional copies of this book may be purchased at $27.95 (plus postage and handling) from

 Hobby House Press, Inc.
1 Corporate Drive, Grantsville, MD 21536
1-800-554-1447
www.hobbyhouse.com
or from your favorite bookstore or dealer.

Printed in the United States of America

ISBN: 0-87588-616-7

The Art of
Making Miniature Millinery

by Timothy J. Alberts, M. Dalton King and
Pat Henry

Introduction

I first came to know Timothy J. Alberts through his designs. It was the perfection of each piece that caught my eye. Not one had anything that could be added, nor one thing that could be left off without disturbing the balance of the creation. In the past, when I have written about his work, I have called Tim's pieces "miniature pieces of art". I have heard others call them "museum pieces". As a student we look for the most knowledgeable of mentors when learning a new skill. In this book, you will find that Tim is not like any other as he is a true master in the art of miniaturization and you, as a student, will be gaining knowledge and skill that will be invaluable in creating your own works of art.

In these pages, you will see creations that will dazzle and delight. Each a perfect miniaturization of real life models. Though as perfect as they may be, it would not be evident without great photography. Pat Henry has been actively honing her skills in this area for the past five years. I have watched while she went from amateur clicker to a finely gifted photographer who is gaining more and more attention for her work. It is through her discerning eye that these pieces are brought to life.

Technique and image come together through Mary King, herself an accomplished writer. With her vivid descriptions and clear instructions, you will be walked through the creation process and in the end be able to make your own beautiful miniatures.

Tim has created all of the hats and clothes in this book as well as several of the dolls on which the hats are displayed. While this instructional guide may seem disguised as a beautiful piece of book art, don't be surprised that when put to use, you too will end up with fabulous creations of beauty.

- Sonia Rivera
Editor and Publisher of the Fashion Doll Scene- www.fashiondollscene.com

Table of Contents

Chloe, in a field of wild flowers. She is dressed in an 18th Century lawn gown and straw hat. Doll and costume created by Timothy J. Alberts

Chapter One-
"Plus ça Change, Plus C'est le Meme Chose"

The more things change the more they stay the same. The same basics, caps, toques, wide brimmed hats, turbans, berets, and hoods have appeared over and over again throughout history, one day the height of fashion, the next relegated to closets and drawers.

The determiner of what shape will take precedence in any particular time is of course, fashion. What the silhouette of the day is, what is happening in a society that will be reflected back in the clothes either as a mirror as has certainly been the case during wars, or, as a counterpoint, as in the 1920's and 1960's when fashion rebelled against a rigidity of mores in society. Or, the prevailing influence could be something as simple as a fad. An item which when presented strikes everyone's fancy and becomes a must have, must wear style for that period of time.

And who creates those things that captures the imagination and creates a general yearning? When it comes to women's hats, it's the milliners. It's their work that has influenced history in ways most people never think of.

Back when, in the year dot, when needs must, hats were created out of necessity, as protection against the elements. It's not hard to imagine a cave-wife ripping a section of fur from a skin and throwing over her husband's head just before he ventured out into the pouring rain to gather dinner. Was that the first, albeit crude, cap, or was it a hood?

Hard to say but it was the beginning of a long tradition of covering the head. For centuries hats just happened.

One person made it, another wore it and others copied it, making it fashion. But again it was an issue of necessity, and not just the elemental kind. It is useful to understand that while hats were, first and foremost, apparel, they were also indicative of class, social standing, the power one held in society, and matters of morality.

That isn't so, now, in the 21st century, but up until the 1970's this was very much the case. No "decent" woman in the 1920's would dream of leaving her home without a hat or her head covered in some fashion, nor in any time before that.

And can you imagine what it what it would be like doing housework wearing a hennin? I'm sure you can't but neither could the women wearing them, nor were they supposed to, for such extravagant headwear would only be worn by the lady of the manor. She who had servants to do the real work. In fact the wearing of a hennin meant there were many things a lady couldn't do.

Women often found themselves restricted, just as they were in their lives, by the clothes they wore, especially hats. An excessively large one could make it difficult to climb into a carriage or car, or do anything at all for that matter. A small one, perched at an angle on your head was always in danger of falling off your head or being blown away by a gust of wind, and required that a woman devote a great deal of thought to her apparel.

Of course the ultimate power "hat" was a crown and the men and women whose heads it graced were, undeniably, at the top of their game. It was to them that the rest of society doffed their hats or stood before them bareheaded, hat in hand. That is, if you were a man.

The doffing of the hat was as much a political statement and recognition of class differences as any custom could be, for it was an issue of "betters". One always doffed one's hat, or cap, to one's betters. A worker to his boss, the boss to an earl, and the earl to a king, or queen. And, depending on the circumstances, after a man had removed his hat, he remained, hat in hand, bareheaded. These practices always "kept men" in their places and were a constant reminder of where they stood on the social scale.

Not quite so for women, for they never doffed their hats. In fact, for centuries, while they did have a distinct place in society, women, for the most part, were never in positions of authority, outside of their homes. Hats for women were worn for protection and, for issues of modesty. Initially it was considered preferential to keep women "under wraps", their hair covered lest it's seductive quality lure a man into unwholesome thoughts.

But the problem was that a wimpled woman was a humble sight and was in no way indicative of the wealth and success her husband or family might enjoy. So veils came off, unless you were a nun, as women became status symbols.

At first, men's hat styles were adapted for women, but slowly, styles were created and came into being that were intended only for the fairer sex. To be sure, there were hat styles that were worn by both men and women, such as the cavalier hats of the 17th century and the tricorne of the 18th century, but for the most part women's hats had a direction that was strictly their own.

It is interesting to note that as men's hats became more sedate and restrained, from the 19th century on, women's hats became more and more imaginative, more and more "designed".

We don't know the names of the people who first made hats; there wasn't even a term to describe their chosen field of work until 1529 when the term "millaner" first appeared. The term was a deviation of Milan, the town in Italy where the some of the finest straw hats and hat making material in the world was available.

Even then it took another 150 years for millinery to become an accepted term for a woman's hat maker and recognized as an art form. Hatters, or haberdashers made hats for men, and even though, there were times, as fashion warranted, that wild concoctions graced their shelves, theirs, for the most part, were staid even somber creations. It was the milliners who began to garner attention and praise.

Starting with Rose Bertin, in the 18th century, the age when the couturier and milliner's work was known and recognized internationally, had begun. She was really the first, and made her fortune from dressing Marie Antoinette from head to toe. First but not the last, for in the centuries that followed, many were to distinguish themselves in this field, Worth, Poiret, Chanel, Schiaparelli, Dior, Givenchy, St Laurent, Halston, and De la Renta to name a

Little Mary learning her ABC's.
Designed by Timothy J. Alberts.

few. Many of these couturiers, as it was with Chanel and Halston, started out as milliners and were eventually inspired to dress the entire woman just as Rose Bertin had. And while they came to be primarily concerned with clothes they never forgot their roots.

The hats they made for their clothes were created to be part of a whole, to compliment the picture, not challenge it. Even Schiaparelli, with her surrealist flair and daring approach, didn't want her hats to take focus and detract from the outfit. Rather they were intended to be the exclamation point at the end of a sentence!

Naturally, there was that who's who soloed with hats and their names are legend. Lily Dasche, Sally Victor, Mr. John, and Paulette, dedicated themselves and their artistry to the creation of hats, daring, outrageous and luscious hats, chic and witty ones, hats which did take focus and those which melted the heart with their beauty. And while, for the most part, hats became superfluous in the 70's and 80's, the tradition has not been lost and has been taken up by the likes of Philip Treacy, John Boyd, and Amy Downs. They continue the tradition started long ago in the 16th century.

Sadly, not every hat is successful at first introduction. There have even been instances when an item of head apparel, such as the top hat, was introduced to general derision and laughter, yet managed to hang on and endure, becoming a symbol of high standard, for over a hundred years.

Men hated the itsy bitsy doll hat of 1938, and no hat has ever been more disparaged than the Empress Eugenie hat of the same decade, but women continued to wear them.

And while here, in this book, our emphasis is on designing and making hats for dolls, a historical perspective is still requisite. For dolls are "us", just a smaller version, perfectly realized. And when designing for a doll, whether it is a Renaissance repro, an 1860's *Bru, Cissy, Gene®, Daisy* and *Willow* or a modern day *Alex*, period accuracy becomes crucial. It's not just an issue of scale, though that is mandatory for a successful design. It's also a question of the eye. For despite the fact that some fashions from times past, may strike us as odd, given our modern conceits, the fact is that due to the influence of movies, books, television and paintings we have all become very well acquainted with how different periods should look. And, as any painter will tell you, it's hard to fool the eye.

For this reason it helps to understand the wheres and why-fors of how a hat is traditionally made, and then translate that process to a miniature scale. Doing exactly that is the purpose of this book.

We will take you, in the following pages and chapters, through the hat making process, demonstrating as we go, three basics: felt,

Buckhouse hat and purse, designed by Timothy J. Alberts.

straw, and, a buckram hat, plus one which is somewhat more complicated, a hat made on a wire foundation. We will discuss why one foundation may be preferable for a particular style over another, how to find, make, or adapt head blocks for small heads. We'll talk about scale and even provide suggestions as to how to re-furbish pre-existing or "store-bought" hats. And, in the visual dictionary, we'll show you what hats were worn when and what they looked like. As a further aid, we try to help you with time and place by categorizing hats.

Certainly more hats have been designed than can be counted; yet some contend there are only two types of hat, brimmed and brimless. And while one could make a case for that point of view or for distinguishing between hats by the foundation material used, straw, felt, wire, fabric or buckram etc., we have found, where dolls are concerned, that it is more helpful to classify hats, by purpose, into the four following categories:

Practical Hats: these are the hats worn everyday, as protection against the elements, for warmth, or as part of one's daily "uniform". If you live in the southwest, a cowboy hat could easily fall into this category, whereas if you live in England, a bowler would be your regular hat. It might seem to present a more formal appearance, but as it is being worn to the office, time and place makes it "everyday". And this is something, which must be taken into account when determining what type of hat is most appropriate for your doll. A large flowered hat might, to modern eyes, suggest an "occasion" but was in reality an everyday hat for a lady of the 1890's. While on the other hand, the hat of a peddler doll will present no such illusions.

One way of differentiating between hats, which are far more special, and those which are not, would be by the materials and trims used for the construction of the hat. Better quality goods, Swiss straws, fine laces, and silk ribbons would be the clue that the hat did not belong in this category but in the one below. For example, a modern doll dressed for a picnic could easily wear a picture hat with flowers, but it would more likely be a hat that one kept on a peg rather than stored in a hatbox.

One additional point needs to be made regarding the wearing of an "everyday" hat in period times and that is this, that here too, the class divide often made itself apparent. For the poorer classes often only had one all purpose hat, a hat that did service for all occasions, quite like Eliza Doolittle's battered one did before Henry Higgins got his hands on her.

Service Hats: the wearing of these hats signifies an association with a particular field or profession. It is easy to identify a member of the armed services, a nurse, a policeman or woman, a construction worker, a member of a fire company, a doorman, bellhop or even a maid simply by the hats they wear.

Dress, Formal, or Occasion Hats: These are the hats one would wear when required to dress up or wear one's best. In modern times this might mean a wedding, some type of formal reception, or even a trip to Ascot. For

Mattel's Audrey Hepburn in a wedding gown and headdress designed by Timothy J. Alberts.

times past, the differentiation is more difficult to discern. There are those, the nobility for example, and those who were famous or had celebrity, who always dressed at the top of their game. This meant top hats for men, and hats that were always beautiful, the epitome of style, and made from the finest fabrics for the women. In the 50's, ladies who lunched made a point of wearing the chicest and finest hats. But these hats would never be worn to grocery store, or merely to pick up one's husband from the train. For most, wearing a hat from this category demonstrates, whether modern or period, a clear divide between the norm and special.

It has been our experience that most doll hats usually fall into this or, the following category. Because dolls are so special, in so many different ways, we often tend to want to give them either an exceptionally beautiful, or, artistic look.

Specialty Hats or Headdresses: This a broad category and can include anything which may be an exception, such as lace caps, mob caps, wimples, hennins, jester caps, cowboy hats made with a flair for a costume, crowns, and ships worn amidst great, wonderful hairdo's. And while lace caps, wimples etc., have been worn in more than one period of time, we consider them to be an exception because of the fact that they weren't universally worn and because they all require construction techniques, which are different than usual. We also include here, fantasy or extraordinary hats, for much the same reasons stated above.

It should be noted, as with all attempts to categorize anything, there are exceptions to the rule. Here, in this book, these would be the crossovers, hats that defy singular classification and belong to more than one category. For example, we might be tempted to place Balenciaga's witty little twig hat in the specialty category, yet at the time it was made, it would certainly have been placed among "dress" hats, of the very smartest sort.

Thus we place an emphasis on time and place, especially when you keep in mind that there were actually times when hats were superfluous.

World War II, had a liberating effect upon women's heads. Hats were still worn but as millinery supplies became harder to come by, going bareheaded became more acceptable. Hats were more often worn for protection rather than glamour. In the 50's and 60's wearing hats became chic again as witty, saucy and frothy confections were offered up for women's heads. But when big, glorious hair, and hairpieces, became most important, in the latter part of the 20th century, hats, as a rule, lost their standing in our society.

Now, in the 21st century, hats are, once again finding a place in our lives. Service and practical hats have never gone away, as our need for them has remained unrelenting since the beginning of time. It is the glamour hats that have come back, the frivolous and silly ones that help define an occasion or personality. For that we are grateful, for fashion seems to have come full circle. And that can only help us, give us a grander scale, a broader canvas when designing for our dolls.

And while, in this book, we stress a need for historical accuracy, an understanding of time and place, paying attention to scale, knowledge of hat making materials and techniques, we don't want you to forget the missing quotient needed. The creativity you bring to the process. This is the fun part of creating a hat, choosing a style, fabric, and color. Should the hat have a veil, flowers, a geometric design, mirrors like Halston once used, a feather or even a bird? Large brimmed or a tiny circle like the swirl hat shown on the introduction page! These decisions are yours, your necessary contribution.

For hats, whether or not we wear them in our own lives, maintain an aura of style, intrigue, fascination, glamour and romance, and should, most definitely, when appropriate, be worn by your doll. To that end, we will begin the hat making process for dolls starting with, chapter 2, The Basics.

Overleaf- Porcelain dolls Rose and Lily enjoy a picnic at "Willow House" in upstate New York. Dolls and costumes by Timothy J. Alberts.

Gene® in the delightful cocktail ensemble, "Charles James",
created exclusively by Timothy J. Alberts.

Barbie® doll "Noir". Mattel's Silkstone Fashion Model Barbie® in black and white buckram hat by Timothy J. Alberts.

16

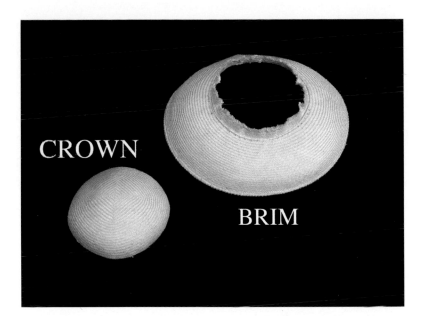

CROWN

BRIM

Chapter Two- The Basics

As with life in general, there are no absolutes when it comes to millinery. What there is is a collective wisdom. Techniques of construction, the basics of foundations, an understanding of what has been found to work best and why. This is the heritage of millinery; knowledge gained through experience, shared, and then passed down, through the centuries, for the benefit of the next generations of milliners. These we will share with you but with a directed emphasis placed on small-scale millinery.

The first step, when making a hat, is often the hardest, for it involves choices and making decisions. What style for what occasion for what person? Keep in mind the period the hat is intended for, what the silhouette of the time was and, the time of year it will be worn. Should the hat be made with a wide brim, as they were in 1909 and again in the 1950's, as a balance to the full skirt? Are you designing for a sleek silhouette, such as the nineteen's when women started to wear tall, narrow hats? Is the dress made from voile, lawn, velvet, or wool? All of these factors are important; for you don't want your hat to overwhelm the doll or the outfit it is wearing.

Scale and proportion will continue to play an important role as you choose fabric, decide on ribbons and trims, and make all the necessary decisions, starting with foundations. What type foundation will best serve the end you desire, felt, buckram, straw, or a wire foundation? For these are the basics.

Let's face it, you can, if you are inventive and creative, make a hat or head covering from just about anything. It certainly has been done; the tin man had a very unique hat, which completely suited his character. The headdresses of showgirls are a complete story in and of themselves, and the platter hats made some decades ago out of vinyl records were definitely an original concept. But you can't go there, to the extreme edge of creativity, without a starting place, a knowledge of the traditional ways of creating the foundations mentioned above. And that is where we will begin.

Most hats, though not all, are made using some type of fabric, and most fabrics do not have the ability to maintain a structured shape. That is the role foundations play in millinery. Made from stiffer materials, such as wire, buckram, straw, and felt, the foundation provides you with the basic shape of your hat. Buckram and wire will then be covered with fabrics and trims of your choice to create a finished look. Straw, for the most part, doesn't get covered, just shaped and trimmed. Felt is the exception in this group, for it is a fabric, albeit a non-woven one, that serves as both the foundation and the hat.

Felt (chapter 4) is one of the oldest fabrics used for hat making. It is said to have been discovered by a monk who put wool on the bottom of his sandals for comfort and found that the combination of the wool, the moisture and warmth from his feet, and the pressure from his body weight made a pliable piece of fabric. A non-woven fabric, felt

Traditionally used for hats designed to be worn in fall and winter, felt hats were always considered to be good protection against inclement weather. They were warm and water has a tendency to bead up and fall off its surface especially if, as it is now in modern times, the felt is sized. How many of you can remember a father, or grandfather, coming in shaking water off his felt fedora?

Felt also offers a great versatility when deciding upon a hat size. It is great for small and large brimmed hats alike. Who can forget the cavalier hats of the 17th century, or the large hats worn by women in the latter half of the 18th century? Felt! Felt which has been blocked, cut, wired or sized, sewn or steamed into shape.

Most felt hats, with very few exceptions, have blocked crowns. These are large pieces of the fabric, which have been placed on the desired sized headblock and steamed into shape. Even the floppy felt hats of the seventies had a blocked crown; it was the brim that was left unstructured. The bell shaped hat of the flapper, in the 1920's, could never have gained such wide public popularity without the versatility of felt, and it's chameleon like ability to adapt to and hold different shapes.

Because of it's solid look, felt hats, even when decorated with ribbons or flowers, have

Madame Alexander's Alex doll putters in her garden wearing a classic straw hat, perfect for a hot day. Designed by Timothy J. Alberts.

often been associated with more somber or serious occasions, such as meetings, business events, funerals or inaugurals. There have even been times when the wearing of a particular type of felt hat was indicative of a certain political affiliation.

Such was the case with the beret in World War II. While it was then, and has remained, the national hat of France, in the war the wearing of those felt, shaped hats, was often a sign that you were a member of the French resistance. Here, in the US, the floppy felt hat became the hat of choice for those who advocated the peace movement in the late 1960's and 70's.

Straw hats (chapter 5) have not had such political attachments; in fact, because of their lighter appearance they are usually worn in spring or summer, and are associated with bright, sunny days, weddings, picnics and summer parties. The quality and look of your hat will be determined by the quality of your straw. Naturally, the finer the straw, the better the hat.

Straw hats are generally made in one of two ways. The first is when the hat is made from straw cloth. The cloth is either blocked into shape, or is made with a combination of cutting, sewing and blocking into the style hat you desire. The second most effective method of making a straw hat is to do so using straw braid as we do in chapter 5.

Hats made with a buckram foundation offer the milliner a great deal of stylistic latitude, as it can be cut, sewn, blocked and shaped into any style hat you can think of. Although buckram is available in 1,2,and 4-ply, you will find that 1 and 2-ply will more than meet your needs. 2-ply is certainly stiff enough to make even the most structured of doll hats, and in most cases 1-ply will be sufficient.

In chapter 3 we will take you through the steps of wetting and stretching the buckram over your block. Buckram, which is a sized, coarse, open weave type of fabric, can usually be found in both black and white, which is a real help as it's easier to effectively cover, and hide buckram when it's color is closer to the shade you are covering the hat with.

Dyeing buckram is a very iffy proposition, for the dyeing process diminishes the sizing

Even the littlest young ladies have co-opted the beret, or tam, as fashionable headwear.

that holds it's shape, and the very reason you used it in the first place. It's best to use the black or white, depending on the color of the hat, and make sure the foundation is completely covered by the fabric. If, you must absolutely have a buckram shape of a particular color, we suggest you paint it lightly once the shape has been determined and assembled, then let it dry completely before covering it with fabric.

The fourth option you have, when making a foundation, is to construct one out of millinery wire. Wire foundations have traditionally been employed for theatrical purposes, or in instances of very high end, very "haute" millinery, and used very little for dolls. But should you desire to make a very light and transparent hat, or one, which has an extreme or unusual shape, this option is one you should definitely consider. Hats made from chiffon, organza, lace and other sheer fabrics usually benefit from a wire foundation for the structure allows you to create a very airy and delicate looking hat, which is the very point of using those types of fabrics.

However, should you choose this method, you will find the need to camouflage the wires. Doing so will prevent the look of the foundation itself from being a distraction, and aid in giving your hat a "finished" look. This can easily be achieved by wrapping the wires with a self-colored chiffon or tulle. You don't want to use too thick a fabric for that would add bulk to a foundation that should remain minimal. You should also be aware that irregardless of the shape of the hat, it needs to be made on a headblock, and then fit on the doll's head before applying fabric, thereby assuring that no matter the shape of the hat, it will fit on your doll's head.

The same wire used above, to make a compete hat, is also used to give a more directed shape to other hats. For instance, it would not be uncommon to sew a thin gauge of millinery wire onto the edge of a felt hat, and then cover it with grosgrain ribbon or bias strips.

A straw that is too floppy for the look you want can be stiffened with the addition of a wire sewn around its brim. The edge, for aesthetic purposes, should then covered, either by folding the straw brim over itself, or by using of straw braid, ribbon, lace, or tulle. And once you have sewn on the wire, and before you finish the hat, place it on your headblock, and check to make sure, the shape of the hat isn't distorted, and the edge flows smoothly.

Headblocks can be a problem when it comes to making hats for dolls. Unlike making hats for humans, you can't just go out and buy a headblock for a doll. They really aren't made, and the few that exist are very hard to come by. You could have canvas ones custom made, or carve one out of wood yourself. But, as doll head sizes are so varied, you'd have to make a block for each and every doll, which could be tiresome.

Our solution is to use pre-existing shapes, and convert them, if necessary, into headblocks. The tops of face cream jars, lids, and the bottom of certain shampoo bottles have all been employed. In fact, a house search is not uncommon when a new hat is being made. It is also our experience, that kitchen and bathroom cupboards yield the best results. When searching try and find a shape that comes closest to the one you are trying to approximate. And remember, the "block" must not be any bigger than the head you are making the hat for. If it is smaller the "block" can be padded out using strips of muslin, thin cotton batting, or by stretching steamed felt over it.

Once you have a "headblock", your next step is to create your pattern. Flat patterning is a very effective method for making a hat. When creating a pattern, we find it helps to have a drawing or picture of the style of hat you want to make, in front of you, to use as a reference. It also makes the process easier, to use a paper which has some body or weight to it, such as card stock, or brown butcher paper, when drawing and cutting out the shapes that will eventually create the foundation for your hat. Heavier paper will be less likely to tear or shred as you work with it, testing your pattern on the headblock. And don't be discouraged if, when trying to get the size and shape right, you have to do it over several times. It is much easier to make corrections at this stage, than when you are further along with the hat.

Once you are satisfied with your pattern pieces, you might consider doing a mock-up of your hat in muslin, or other such fabric. This extra step could be a time saver, in the long run, for it will ensure that the hat does indeed fit your doll, and that it's scale and proportion are "pleasing" to your eye. Making a mock-up has the added benefit of saving fabric, a real plus if you are using vintage, or special ribbons or lace.

It should be pointed out that if you are using a wire foundation, or creating an extraordinarily shaped hat, doing a muslin may not be an option, trial and error being

your only recourse. But please don't let this scare you off any project, for the shapes you will be dealing with are so small that, unlike with human sized heads, guesstimating can prove beneficial. In fact, having to repeat a process a few times is often a blessing for it can lead to greater precision in your work.

At this point your major decisions have been made. You've chosen a style, picked the foundation you think will best suit the end you are trying to achieve, made your pattern and are ready to begin making your foundation, and finally your hat. This would be an appropriate time to discuss some of the supplies you'll need on hand or may find helpful to have around, just in case.

The list will be on the short side, composed primarily of what we think is absolutely essential, as well as obtainable. For the sad fact is that the availability of millinery supplies is on the decline, and has been for nearly 20 years.

It started in the 1970's, when the wearing of hats became less popular, and no longer a common sight on heads. Fewer hats were sold, fewer hats became made and a smaller number of people became milliners. Thus the need for millinery supplies dwindled. They can still be found, but doing so may involve a search. If you can find a place that still has old supplies buy up all you can, for they are treasures. Now, not all the materials you use will be hard to find, some are easily obtainable as they can be found in notions stores. But we'll tell you, as we go down the list, what is available, what can be harder to find, and where possible, suggest suitable alternatives. The following are the items you should have on hand:

*Some simple objects to create hats upon include jars and lids, as
well as ready made hat blocks.*

Your doll - *Your model, check the hat on the
head it's being made for, from time to time.*

A picture or drawing - *Of the style hat you
are planning to make.*

Headblock - *Barring the possibility of having
a custom canvas or wooden block made in the
size and shape of your doll's head, look
around your home for a suitable alternative.*

*Make sure the substitute is the same size or
smaller than your doll's head, is stable
enough to withstand tugging and pulling, and
can accommodate the size and shape of the
foundation you are making. Your "headblock"
should also have enough length to it that it
will allow you to stretch your fabric down. As
you will learn in the relevant chapters (3 &
4), this is important, especially when working
with felt and buckram for the stretching down*

of the foundation, after it has been secured to the block, will give you a smooth surface upon which to make your hat. Luckily, because doll heads are so much smaller than humans, we're talking about inches here.

Paper - As mentioned above, cardstock or brown butcher or wrapping paper would be best, or any paper which has enough strength to withstand any tugging and pulling it may receive as you check to see that your patterns conform to the shape you are seeking.

Tape - You'll find this very handy to have on hand when making your paper pattern. In essence you will end up making a paper hat and you will need tape if you want to make changes, like adding length to a shape that is too short, or just keeping the shape of the paper model together, to try it out.

Pencils and pens - Sharpened pencils and fine-point pens are needed to draw your pattern pieces and mark levels on your foundation. If you are working with a dark colored felt or buckram, a white pencil will make it easier for you to see the lines you've drawn.

Assorted needles - The type of hat you are making will determine the size needle you use. Finer fabrics will obviously need a thinner needle, whereas when sewing on felt and buckram, a heavier needle is called for. Obviously, milliner's needles would be a plus for they are long, thin, and flexible, can pierce even the toughest fabrics and easily sew around a small circle.

Pins - You will find that pins are essential when pinning pattern and hat piece together and, trim to the hat. If your block is soft enough you can also pin the hat to it while you are working on it. An extra little tip, if you are working with a wonderful silk and are afraid of the holes straight pins sometimes leave in fabric, use needles as a substitute, they are much thinner and less likely to leave a mark.

Assortment of thread - You'll need colors and strengths of thread to accommodate your foundation and fabrics. Again, the finer the material the lighter the weight of threads needed, and vice versa.

A piece of beeswax - Run the beeswax down your length of thread before sewing to give it added strength and protect it from fraying and breaking. This really helps when sewing buckram.

Assorted scissors - Fabric scissors, coarser scissors for cutting buckram, and those with fine points to cut into small areas, will all be needed. And if you have a rare pair of scalloping shears and are creating a very "decorative" hat, place those on your worktable as well.

Assorted rulers and curves - For making the patterns. The curves will be especially helpful as all brims are curved.

Measuring tape - To measure the doll's head, and your headblock.

Glues - These are used to adhere fabrics to foundations, to glue sections of the hat together, and to attach trims such as feathers and flowers to the hat. Timothy primarily uses 3 types of glues for his millinery; Sobo, which is a wonderful adhesive that has the added benefit of not bleeding through and ruining the look of fabrics, Magna-tac, which bonds very quickly and dries clear, and, spray adhesives which are good to temporarily attach fabric to buckram before stitching it in place. Securing the fabric this way makes it easier to maintain the desired shape while working on the hat without softening the fabric itself. A fourth glue which is a help when gluing fabric to buckram, and you find the spray adhesive isn't strong enough, is Rubber Cement. It is particularly effective for work on curved and convex areas of the brim.

Cotton batting, muslin strips, or felt - To pad out the headblock, if necessary.

Fabric - To cover your hat, your choice. Also, do you want the hat lined? You'll also need fabric for that.

Felt - Chapter 4 provides a more in-depth discussion of felt.

Straw - Do you plan on using cloth or braid? See chapter 5.

Seam ripper - For obvious reasons.

Sewing machine - If your hat isn't absolutely teeny, use a machine where you can. Doing so ensures that your stitches are strong and have a uniform length.

Iron - Good for pressing both pattern and fabric pieces if needed, and a few puffs of steam can give your hat a nicely finished touch. However, when actually making the hat you would be wise to press as you go, for it won't be possible to press it completely once the hat is finished.

Small steamer - If you need more steam than your iron can provide a small steamer is an excellent piece of equipment to have on hand. If you don't have one, a teakettle is an alternative you can use to remove any wrinkles and smooth out your hat. Be careful not to get the fabric to close to the kettle, to prevent the fabric from getting too wet or burned. We sometimes make a funnel out of aluminum foil and attach it to the end of the spout to prevent damage to the fabric. Felt, especially the heavier weights don't burn easily and usually benefits from a good steam.

Buckram - If needed, see chapter 3

Millinery wire - There are 3 types of wires you should have on hand when making a hat. Wires are basically used to stabilize the edge of a foundation shape or brim of a hat. But, if you want to give a saucy little twist or angle to a brim, you will definitely need to have wired the edge. The first wire is simply

> Beautiful ribbons can create a new and different style for each hat you design, no matter what foundation you base yours upon.

referred to as Millinery Wire. A finer gauge wire (#21) usually suffices for doll hats, but it wouldn't hurt to have #19 (heavier gauge) on hand just in case your requirements change or the doll you are creating a hat for is exceptionally large. And if you are creating a wire foundation you'll need Tie Wire, which is a very thin metal wire, comes on a spool and is used to tie the joins of millinery wire, as well as joining the edging and head wires. A third wire that you should have is Cloth Wire. Cloth wire is a fine, flexible wire, which is wrapped in cotton, is available in either white or green and comes on a very small spool. It is generally used for wiring flowers or other hat embellishments, but it has yet another use. When creating a hat for a doll with a very small head, such as Barbie, this wire adapts itself more easily, than regular millinery wire, to the scale of a tiny hat.

Needle-nose pliers - *To pull reluctant needles through difficult fabrics. This will cut down on the wear and tear of your fingers.*

Wire cutters - *To cut the millinery wire.*

Cotton flannel - *Often used on hats to minimize the outline of wire foundations, used in the mulling process (see glossary).*

Silk organza - *To be used as a press cloth for an iron which should never be directly placed on straw or felt.*

Sizing - *Simply called hat sizing and found at millinery supply stores, Best to spray this on with the windows open as it's very heady stuff.*

When sprayed, sizing will stiffen and stabilize buckram or felt, thus helping to retain your hat shape. However, this sizing doesn't absorb into the fabric, and when sprayed will remain on the surface. For this reason we suggest you spray the sizing on the inside, or the interior of the hat.

Dye - *Just in case you need a specific color. Bear in mind that dyeing removes sizing, which you will have to replace. Also, particularly with felt, make sure that the dye you use does the job completely and doesn't leave any speckles. We suggest dyeing a small sample first. Completely submerge the felt in the dye, allowing enough time for the fabric to absorb it thoroughly. Also, in our experience, felt dyes best when it has been completely soaked in water first. This soaking makes the felt more soluble and able to better absorb the dye.*

Needle board - *When working on velvet, velveteen, or fabrics with a pile, using a needle board protects the nap from being mashed.*

Grosgrain ribbon - *Matched to the color of the hat, finishes the edge of a brim nicely. It can also be used for a hatband.*

Trims- *Ribbons, flowers, feathers, bows, anything you want to use to decorate your hat.*

Rubber bands - *To secure your wet, or damp, foundation to your block, after it has been stretched. Leave the rubber band on until the foundation dries.*

Floral Tape - *To cover and "beautify" the wires on flowers.*

Watercolors - *When you create a hat using a wire foundation, a neat trick is to paint the fabric that covers the wires with watercolors. Choose a color that matches the fabric you are going to cover the hat with, and you'll find that one or two applications of the watercolor will go a long way in camouflaging the wire. Just be sure the paint has dried completely before going onto the next step.*

You have your doll, your design, and all your supplies assembled. You are now ready to begin making a hat. Depending on whether you are making a straw, felt, buckram, or hat with a wire foundation, your next step is to go the appropriate chapter for instructions and a demonstration.

As a reference, for the following chapters, we show 2 hats that are unassembled. The first, one made from straw cloth with a blocked crown is at the beginning of the chapter. On that hat there is the rounded tip of the hat, the sideband beneath the tip (combined these two are called the crown), the collar, which is where the crown and brim are attached, and the head opening.

The second, a standard shape used for many hats, is made from buckram. All the parts are named, which should help you as you read the next four chapters and, then, begin to make your first hat using the techniques offered in this book.

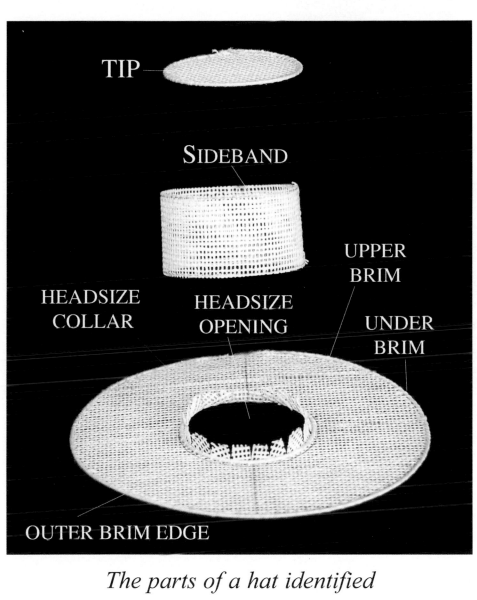

The parts of a hat identified

TIP

SIDEBAND

HEADSIZE COLLAR

HEADSIZE OPENING

UPPER BRIM

UNDER BRIM

OUTER BRIM EDGE

29

Ashton Drake's Gene® enjoying a brief respite in the park, with Louis and Cosette.
Costume and dogs designed and created by Timothy J. Alberts.

Chapter Three-
Buckram Hats

When you want, or need, to make a very shaped hat for your doll, using buckram for your foundation is an ideal solution. You'll also find that if you want to create a hat from a really light or transparent fabric, such as organza and lace, using buckram for your foundation is an excellent option. It lends itself to the process beautifully, and eliminates the need to do a completely wired foundation, which can be tiresomely difficult and tricky.

Buckram is a very interesting "material"! When dry and in its' natural state it is as stiff as a board, but when wet, it can be shaped or stretched to any shape you choose. And, then, when dry, it becomes stiff again and successfully retains its new shape. You should be aware however, that because of these very properties, buckram hats cannot be steamed or wet in any way once the desired shape is achieved.

Composed of an open weave fabric, buckram is usually sold in black or white. Colors are rare and difficult to come by. Dyeing really isn't an option because, as stated in Chapter 1, the dyeing process will eliminate the very sizing, which is so essential to the making, and the retaining of, the shape of the foundation. Your best bet, in this case, is to make sure that whatever fabric you use to cover the shape does it well enough to camouflage the buckram. Of course there is always the option of painting the buckram with the desired color once it has been blocked and stretched to the desired shape.

You will also find that, even when working in a miniature size, either one or two-ply buckram will work equally well. Two-ply, if you can find it, is really quite helpful for the finer weave side makes it easier to more accurately mark your patterns, and helps prevent the edge of the buckram from shredding as you stitch. As far as other the supplies you'll need, you will find a list of the basics in chapter 2.

In this chapter a pillbox hat is demonstrated. These hats have never really gone out of style since Jackie Kennedy made them so popular. Using this classic shape has an additional advantage, besides being a good model to demonstrate the technique of working with buckram; it can also be translated into a toque, the beginning of a turban, and the fundamental part of a brimmed hat. The scarf hats of the 1940's were created around a pillbox shape, as were the toques of the 1870's.

The pillbox demonstrated here is for *Barbie®*.

A lovely vintage titian bubblecut Barbie® doll wears the hat demonstrated in this chapter. Liz wears a variation of a buckram hat as bridesmaid, for a change!

We will begin by demonstrating how to stretch buckram over a "headblock" (in this case the headblock being a perfume bottle) or hat shape, cover the hat with fabric and, finally, finish it off.

After we have given an example of how to make a hat, which has a blocked buckram shape, we then provide you with an example of a buckram hat that has been made from flat patterned pieces of buckram and covered with fabric to create a Victorian hat for a doll named Emily. We show you how to make the pattern, transfer it to buckram, and then once you have the foundation of the hat, how to proceed and, finish it off.

We have also included a sample of a third hat, a constructed hat of a more common shape than Emily's hat. While we provide a synopsis, rather than showing you the entire

hat step by step, we think, given the previous paragraphs you should have no trouble understanding how we started with a different buckram shape and ended up with a completely different hat. In fact, with the basics demonstrated here you should be able to adapt the techniques and use them to make any buckram hat. So we'll begin with the first of these, the pillbox for *Barbie®*.

1. *To begin, there are a few standard tips it will help you to know. They will come in handy regardless of the hat you are making. The first of these is called "springing the wire", which means you straighten the wire by pressing the wire with the padded portion of your thumb against the curve of the wire. The reason you do this is so that when you sew your wire to your buckram, or felt, it won't twist as you sew it. For if it does twist, it will distort the foundation piece you are working on, making it necessary to undo your work and start again.*

2. *You'll find it immensely helpful, to establish the center-front and center back, as soon as possible on your hat. All wires, bindings and trims etc., will begin and end at the center back.*

3. *The proper way to cut millinery wire is to use wire cutters, straight onto the wire, (see demonstration picture), and the proper way to bend the wire is to use needle-nose pliers and press as demonstrated.*

4. *There are three stitches you will use with your millinery foundation. The first is a blanket stitch. With this stitch you insert the needle into buckram, over the wire and pass it through the loop that is formed and then make your next stitch.*

5. *The second stitch is the one you will probably use most often for it leaves less of a ridge than other stitches, a plus for doll millinery. The whipstitch is very simple, just pass the needle through the buckram, over the wire, and then repeat the movement along the length of the wire.*

6. *The stab stitch is passed over the wire, through the buckram in a straight up and down motion.*

7. *When sewing hats, waxing your thread gives a greater strength as well as ease to your thread. To do so, run a piece of beeswax down the length of your thread. After you have coated the thread with the wax, press it with a warm iron, which will melt the wax into the thread.*

The Barbie® hat is a blocked buckram hat.

8. *First cover your headblock with aluminum foil, and over that place a layer of plastic wrap, which will make it easier to remove the buckram from the block.*

9. *Then cut- a large enough square of buckram to cover your headblock (in this case a perfume bottle) and extend down several inches, all the way around.*

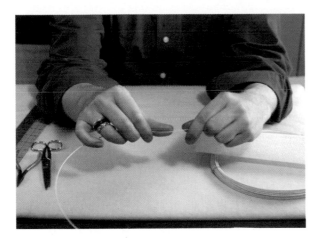

fig.1- Springing the wire

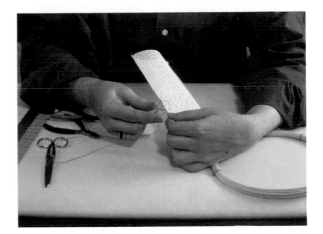

fig.4- The blanket stitch

fig.2- cutting the millinery wire

fig.5- The whip stitch

fig.3- Bending the wire

fig.6- The stab stitch

fig.7- Perfume bottle as hat block

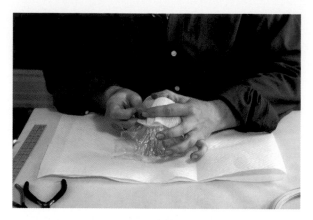

fig.10- Smoothing the buckram over your block

fig.8- Covering the bottle with foil and plastic wrap

fig.11- Secured buckram, stretched smoothly over the block

fig.9- Wetting the buckram

fig.12- Marking dried shape

10. Immerse the buckram in a bowl of luke-warm water making sure it is completely submerged. Let it sit 2 seconds, until the buckram begins to soften.

11. Remove the buckram from the water and lay it on the form. Smooth it over your block, and secure it with a rubber band or elastic tie.

12. Working your way around the edge of the buckram, keep pulling and stretching it until your shape is completely smooth and wrinkle free. A wrinkle in the buckram will put a wrinkle in your hat.

13. Allow the buckram to dry completely, making especially sure that the area where the buckram has been tied has also dried.

14. Mark your cutting edge. That is, where you want the edge of your hat to be.

15. Remove the buckram from the block.

16. Trim the buckram, cutting it where you made the mark.

17. Your next step will be to wire the edge of your hat form. This is done to strengthen and stabilize the buckram form. Because the Barbie® hat is so small we suggest using cloth wire (see glossary), which is a much thinner wire than millinery wire.

18. Using a tape measure around the bottom of the hat form, determine the amount of wire you will need, adding enough of an overlap to make a secure join but not so much as to make it bulky. Then cut the wire from the spool.

19. Make the shape you need with the cloth wire and starting in the center of the overlap, begin to wrap tie wire around the join. Trim the excess tie wire and then using the needle-nose pliers, crimp the join to smooth it.

20. Attach the wire shape to the buckram form using a whipstitch. Take care, as you sew, that the needle and thread don't shred the buckram. For the photos, we used black thread on white buckram, just for the sake of visibility. Ordinarily you would use a matching color thread. And, for these small, fine hats we suggest using quilting thread, which is both very fine, and strong.

21. Place the hat shape on the headblock to make sure its shape hasn't become distorted.

22. It is at this point that you will need to know what you want your hat to look like. The sample we are doing is going to be left in its raw state. If you want a different color you can paint it, but knowing that moisture can weaken your foundation this will have to be done very lightly. But should you decide to paint your foundation, you should place your shape on your headblock before painting it.

23. Decide what you are going to cover your hat with and begin that process.

24. For our sample the next step is to bind the edge with a bias strip of lightweight batiste, which is ideal for such a small hat. To do this use glue, gluing and stretching the edge as you go to get as smooth an edge as possible. Let the glue dry completely. And because we are doing a very basic covering, it would look best if the bias edge shows as little, and is as narrow as possible, because we are not going to line the sample hat.

25. The next step is covering the hat. You can use net, as we have here, tulle, or draped fabric as has been done with the Elizabeth Taylor doll in the bridesmaid outfit. If you make the hat from draped fabric it's best to do it on the headblock or head the hat is being made for.

26. Keep checking your hat on the headblock to make sure it hasn't lost its shape.

27. For the sample hat, 4 layers of millinery veiling could be used. We use eight, which gives it an even more "intense" look. You can change colors or even the density of colors just by adding layers.

28. Pin the net on and start to shape it over your buckram foundation. Then you will stab stitch the fabric on. Make sure if you're using veiling that you catch enough to keep it securely in place. A single thread in the needle will suffice, for such a lightweight material.

29. After the veiling has been stitched and trimmed, if there are any little areas that haven't been caught, just use a little Magna-tac to glue any frayed ends down.

30. The next step is to bind the edge with a decorative ribbon. For the sample we use 3/8" navy grosgrain ribbon. The one we use is a cotton/rayon blend, which is the best grosgrain you can use for millinery. It can be pressed and keep shapes, it can be ironed into circles, can be used for binding the bottom or used for a headband (or sweatband as it is sometimes called). Polyester ribbon is not acceptable for this process.

31. Press the ribbon in half. Apply it by folding over the edge and stitching it on, making sure the ribbon covers all raw edges. The outside and the inside are sewn together at the same time. This will finish off the hat eliminating the need for a lining or headband.

32. Now your hat is ready to be decorated or trimmed. Your trim can be anything you wish, bows, jewels, and flowers. The sample has been covered with small bows made from satin ribbons that have been glued on. Pearls have been stitched to the bows and hat body.

33. A nice finishing touch is to put a small label or bow at the center back of the interior of the hat. This step also lets the customer or doll know what the intended center back of the hat should be.

fig.13- Removing dried buckram shape

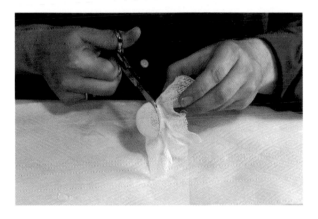

fig.14- Trimming the buckram

fig.15- Final shape ready for wiring

fig.16- Tie wire used to join the cloth wire ring to the buckram

fig.17- Forming cloth wire into an edging circle

fig.18- The completed join on the edge wire

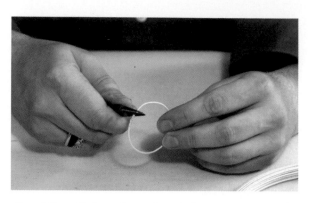

fig.19- Crimping the join to neaten it

fig.22- Checking for distortion of the hat foundation

fig.20- Placing the wire on the edge prior to stitching

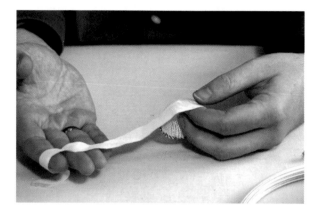

fig.23- The bias batiste strip

fig.21- The wiring of foundation completed.

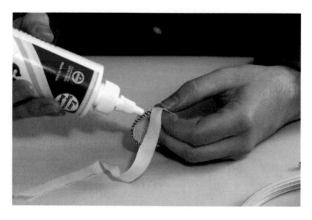

fig.24- Gluing the edging

fig.25- Stretching bias for smooth fit

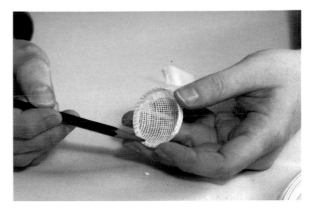

fig.28- Keep your bias edge as narrow as possible

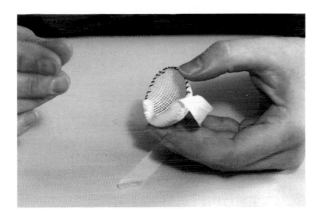

fig.26- Covering the outside and inside evenly

fig.29- Covering the hat with four layers of net

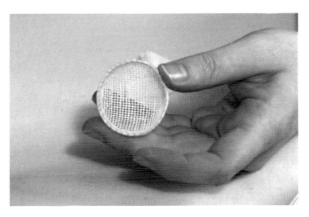

fig.27- Completed binding

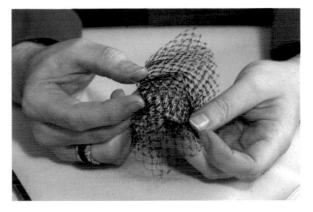

fig.30- Covering the hat with eight layers of net

fig.31- Stitching net into place

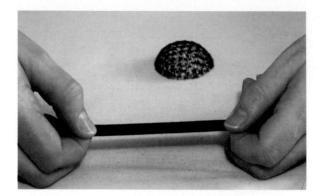

fig.34- Grosgrain for finished binding

fig.32- Trimmed net

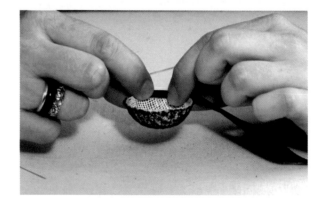

fig.35- Folding binding equally over edge

fig.33- Affixing loose fibres in place

fig.36- Stitching both sides

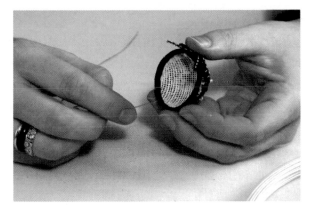

fig.37- Binding neatly and finishing the interior

fig.39- Or bow!

fig.38- Marking center back with a label

fig.40- Hat finished and trimmed

fig.41- A draped version of the same hat

34. Looking inside the finished hat you can see how neat it looks, no raw edges, no stitches showing. Truly a desired result for a creation that has taken some amount of thought and work.

Liz's Bridesmaid Hat

The peach silk hat *Liz* wears for the wedding picture was made the same way as the Barbie® hat above. A similar blocked crown of buckram was made and edge-wired. The edge was bound and the hat was draped in peach silk. The hat was then decorated with sewn on peach beads and a bias bow.

Audrey's Bridal Headdress

The bridal headdress for *Audrey* was made the same way as *Liz's*, with a few differences. The blocked crown was cut shorter, and then a sideband of buckram was sewn to the crown. Both the crown and sideband were then covered and then a flat bias bow and veiling were added.

Emily's Hat

The hat for *Emily* is an 1830's "romantic" hat from the early part of the Victorian era. It is a flat patterned hat, which means that it is made with a drafted pattern rather than a draped one. Inches, quarter inches, and the angle of a curve will be important here. The thing about making flat patterns is that it is a skill that can be either acquired by taking a pattern drafting class, or by trial and error. Fortunately, doll heads are small which makes the trial and error route less of a problem, for often the changes are miniscule, and the adjustments easily made on your original patterns. That is where we will begin, with the paper pattern.

1. With a picture or sketch of the style hat you plan to make, in front of you, begin the process by drawing preliminary shapes on heavy paper.

2. The pattern for Emily's *hat was worked out on the doll's head, with the doll completely dressed and wigged. This was done to ensure that the proportions of the hat would be correct in relation to the head and clothes.*

3. Another consideration that was taken into account when making the pattern for this hat was, though they had very large brims, fashion plates from the time show that the face and lot of the hair was visible at the top of the hat. Now if you made the hat exactly as the "profile" of a period pattern might dictate, because you are doing it for a doll, you could lose the overall look needed for the silhouette. To compensate for that, the paper pattern was adjusted to make the face more visible. The head opening at the top of the crown was also raised for the same purpose while the necessity for a graceful sweep of the brim was kept in mind.

4. *The adjusted pattern, which has been taped together, shows the face while maintaining a graceful brim.*

5. *After adjusting and refining the paper pattern, cut the pieces out of cardstock or heavy paper. Establish the center front and center back of the pattern with pencil or pen. It also helps if, right at the beginning, you write on the pattern what the pattern is for and what each individual piece is.*

6. *The pattern pieces are then laid on the buckram and traced out in pencil. The only place where you will put a seam allowance is at the edge of the brim that fits on the crown of the hat and on one side of the center back of the sideband.*

7. *The center-front mark you made established the grain line. Cut the buckram on the straight grain, because it is a woven material.*

8. *Overlap the center back of the sideband and stab stitch in place.*

9. *The next step is to measure out your millinery wire (remember to spring it) before edge wiring the various pieces of the hat.*

10. *The tip gets wired on the edge using a whipstitch and quilting thread that has been coated with wax. When edge wiring*

the tip, you have to trim away a little of the buckram, for wiring the edge will make the tip a little larger.

11. *The interior of the brim, the head edge that goes into the crown, which is called the head wire, it is placed on the lines you have drawn and stab stitched into place. You will then edge the brim after the hat has been put together. Neither edge of the sideband is wired.*

12. *Whipstitch the tip to the top of the sideband, carefully, so as not to tear through the buckram.*

13. *Notch the seam allowance on the inside head opening of the brim. Bend them upwards and slip into the head opening of the sideband, matching center-front to center-front. Pin in place and securely stitch.*

14. *Make a circle of wire, of the correct length for the brim edge, and join it together using a tie wire. Then bend it into the shape of the brim edge. Lay the shaped wire on the brim and edge stitch it in place.*

15. *After the hat has been wired it needs to be bound with muslin strips to blur the hard edge of the wire and the stitches, which could show through any soft, shiny fabric you might use for the cover.*

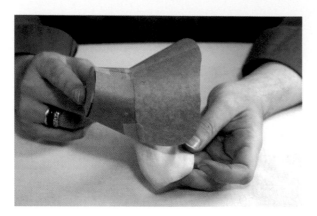

fig.1- Making initial paper pattern

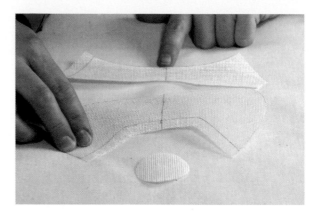

fig.4- Pattern transferred to buckram and cut out with seam allowance added and center front marked

fig.2- Final corrected paper pattern

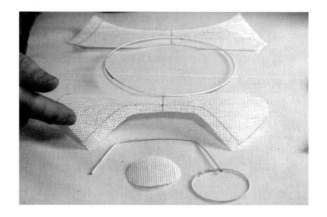

fig.5- Buckram and wire pieces ready for assembly.

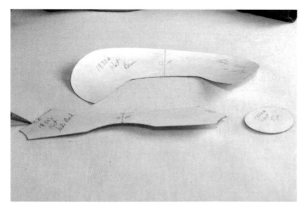

fig.3- Paper pattern transferred to card stock

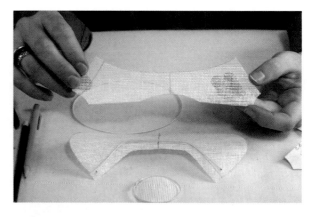

fig.6- Buckram side band showing overlap on one edge at center back

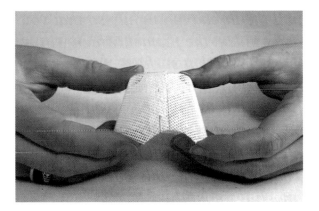

fig.7- Side band pinned and ready
for stitching

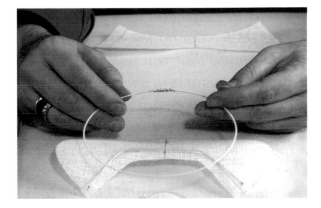

fig.10- Brim wire circled and joined
with tie wire

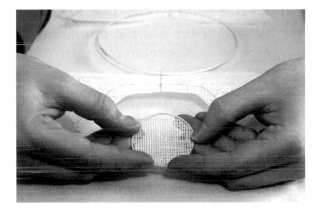

fig.8- Edge wire placed on tip ready
for stitching

fig.11- Shaped brim wire

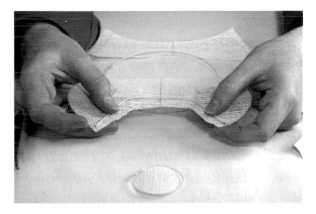

fig.9- Head wire placed in position
ready for stitching

fig.12- Binding the join of tip to the
side band

47

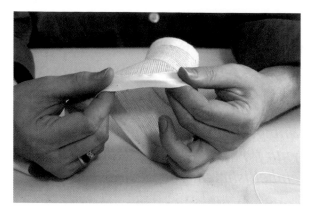

fig.13- Stretching and gluing binding on brim edge over wire

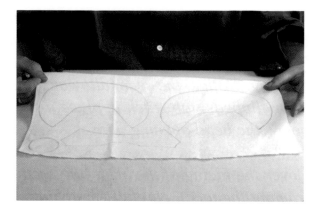

fig. 16- Pattern pieces traced on flannel

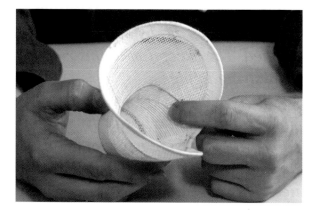

fig.14- Showing bound shape with head wire in place, ready to begin mulling

fig.17- Applying flannel to interior of brim

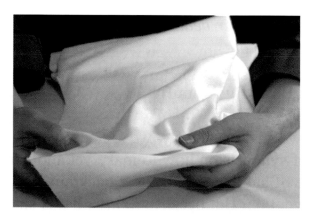

fig.15- Baby flannel for mulling

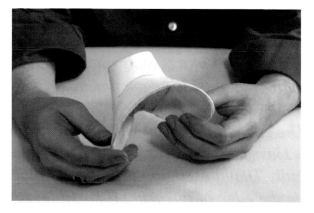

fig.18- Mulling process completed, hat is ready to be covered

period specific hat, we think it is important for you to see how a more "commonly" shaped hat is made. If you want to make a more basic hat, you may find this an easier way to accomplish your goal.

1. *Begin by making your pattern and buckram foundation.*

2. *Just as with* Emily's *hat, start by covering the tip of the crown, as smoothly as possible.*

3. *Then lie on the upper brim section and pin it in place starting at the center-front going around one side to the center-back and then the other side to the center- back. Make sure the fabric is laying smoothly,*

4. *Pin the head opening at the same time.*

5. *Turn the seam allowance over the wired edge to the under side of the brim. Sew it down to the muslin binding.*

6. *Next, cover the under brim in the same way, carefully pinning it in place, starting at the center-front and moving around the hat.*

7. *The under brim fabric is then stitched to the covering of the upper brim which has been turned under. Then it is turned into the crown and stitched.*

8. *To finish the crown, you need a bias piece of the covering fabric.*

9. *Stretch it around the sideband of the foundation, and carefully slip stitched in place, to the tip, and, stab stitched to the head size opening.*

10. *The closure is placed at a position that will be concealed by the trim, or, it could simply be placed at the center back.*

11. *Trim your hat any way you choose, then line the inside of the crown and add the headband.*

Emily's Finished Hat

fig.19- Same pattern pieces used to cut covering fabric

fig.22- Side band top seam allowance neatly tucked

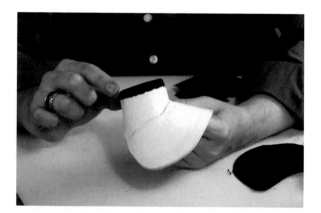

fig.20- Tip covered and smoothly stitched in place

fig.23- Covering pinned in preparation to stitch to tip

fig.21- Stitch center back seam of side band covering

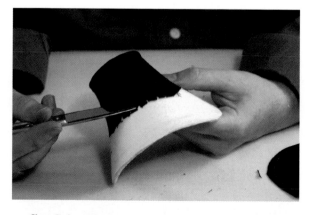

fig.24- Bottom edge of side band seam allowance notched to fit brim

fig.25- Smoothing outside brim cover in place

fig.28- Drawstring lining

fig.26- Outer brim cover pinned in place

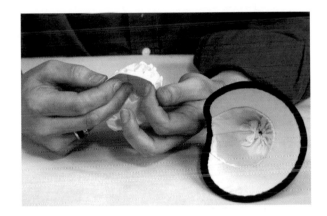

fig.29- Fitted taffeta lining

fig.27- Stitching outer brim cover in place

fig.30- Fitted lining in place before stitching

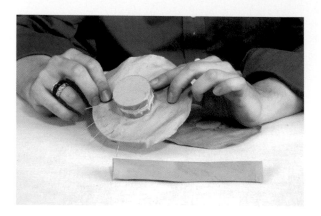

fig.1- Tip covered and sewn in place

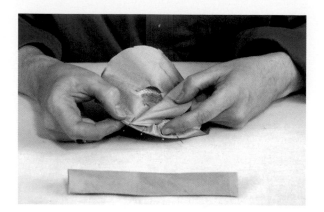

fig.3- Under brim covering pinned
to seam allowance of upper brim
covering

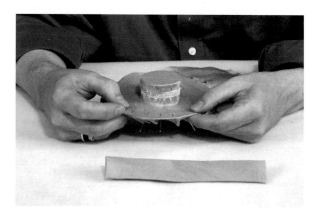

fig.2- Upper brim sewn in place

fig.4- Bias side band in place, ready
for stitching

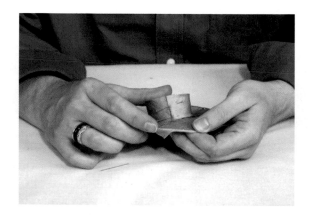

fig.5- Center back seam in place
before stitching

Basic Black on Louis.
Buckram hat trimmed with grosgrain and ribbon, by Timothy J. Alberts.

Ashton Drake's Madra Lord prepares to mourn in style,
wearing Timothy J. Alberts "Requiem"

Chapter Four- Felt Hats

Felt has been used for making hats for just about as long as humans have been wearing them. Made from fur, wool, or a blend of wools and at times, cotton, or, as becoming more and more common, synthetics, felt is mixed with water to break down the fibers and then steamed and pressed into a pliable fabric. It has a further advantage in that it doesn't have a straight grain, which means that felt can be stretched in any direction, which makes it more economical and flexible to use. Felt also, once it has been steamed and blocked, retains it shape well and has a tendency, depending on the type felt you use, to repel water.

The best felt is, of course, fur felt. Rare and difficult to find these days, it is made from rabbit, raccoon or beaver fur. This is the most sumptuous felt. It dyes beautifully, keeps it shape wonderfully and, when made up into a hat, has a lustrous sheen. Fur felt also has the water repellant aspect that was so treasured by those who were exposed to the elements daily and for whom umbrellas weren't always an option.

A wonderful example of hats made from fur felt were the beaver hats so favored by the Quakers in the 18th century, and which, subsequently became the height of fashion. The top-hat, worn by men in the 19th century, was preferred because they were also made of beaver and had the lovely luster which marked it as a hat of distinction. In fact they were often referred to simply as a "beaver".

The wide-brimmed hats women wore throughout the 17th and 18th century, as well as the hats of the 1890's the turn of the century, the teens, and the 20's were often made from fur felt, for the very reasons mentioned above.

Fur felt, as stated previously, is hard to come by these days, though a good source is old human sized hats that can be found in flea markets and secondhand stores and then re-cycled into smaller hats for dolls. However, if you don't have the time or inclination to find fur felt your best recourse is the second type of felt used for better hats, good wool felt.

Usually made from mohair or sheep's wool, this felt has the same properties as fur felt in that it can be stretched in any direction, effectively blocked into any hat shape, and

Alex wears a retro inspired spiral suit, with matching felt hat, designed by Timothy J. Alberts.

will retain that shape, especially when sized, under most conditions. It dyes well and, unless you are in an absolute deluge, wool felt will repel water.

Today, the most common felt used, and the least expensive, is a blend of some wool combined with either rayon or cotton. It is easy to produce, and will retain the shape of the hat, if you use a heavy enough weight, but not as well as it would if you used a wool felt. Something you should also be aware of is that the combo felts are not as stable as fur or wool felt and have a tendency to pull apart during the blocking process. Another shortcoming of these combo felts is that they don't dye as well as other felts, and the colors achieved aren't as brilliant or clear. In addition, because cotton and rayon is water absorbent, these felts won't protect you, or the hat itself, if you should find yourself in a storm or shower.

Another possibility, available in some stores, is velour felt. Also made from wool, this felt has longer, velvet-like nap, which is ideal for making period hats.

We should also mention that there is polyester felt on the market but as it can't be blocked, it's useless for our purposes.

Felt is available in different weights, or thickness. For doll making, you will generally find that it is easier to work with a lighter weight felt. Not so thin that it tears when you block it nor looks insubstantial when you need a serious period hat, but thin and pliable enough that you can easily shape the felt into a miniature hat.

In this chapter the hat being demonstrated, is a black felt 1950's hat, which Tim designed as part of an outfit named, "Requiem" and was made for a doll to wear to a funeral.

With the re-creation of the "Requiem" hat, we take you through the necessary steps involved with the making of a felt hat. Using this guideline, you should be able to transfer the basics acquired here to the making of any style felt hat.

And although the hat was originally black, we have decided to use red for the demonstration. We thought it might make it easier to see the progression of the how-to steps.

1. *This hat has a blocked felt crown that has been edge wired and then attached to a brim. To begin...*

2. *As the crown is blocked, the only pattern you need is for the brim.*

3. *Once you have a paper pattern, try it on the doll's head or a head of the correct size.*

4. *Trace the paper pattern onto the felt.*

5. *Cut out the brim.*

Chloe, dressed in her winter finery, sports a felt tricorne, popular for ladies as well as men in the 18th century. Designed by Timothy J. Alberts.

6. *The original has a feather as a decoration. If you wish to have the same look, punch the feather holes into the brim. It is much easier to do it at this stage rather than when the hat is completely made.*

7. *Choose a headblock that is the right size for your doll's head and cover it first with aluminum foil and then plastic wrap. Cut a square of the felt you are using for the crown, making sure you have allowed*

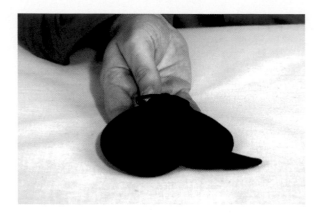

fig.1- Felt hat made of separate
blocked crown and flat brim

fig.4- Hat brim holes punched prior
to cutting out

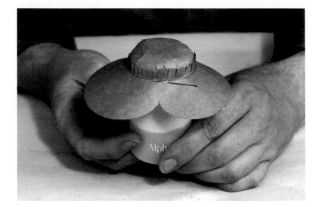

fig.2- Paper pattern used to establish
proper dimensions

fig.5- Dampening felt with steam
before blocking

fig.3- Brim pattern drawn onto felt
and cut out

fig.6- Felt centered on block and
secured with elastic

fig.7- Steaming and stretching felt

fig.10- Trimmed and blocked crown

fig.8- Felt stretched to remove all wrinkles above elastic

fig.11- Crown edge wired with millinery wire

fig.9- Cutting edge, measured and marked

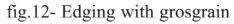

fig.12- Edging with grosgrain

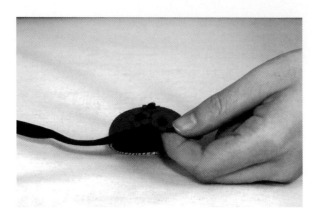

fig.13- Possible trim finish

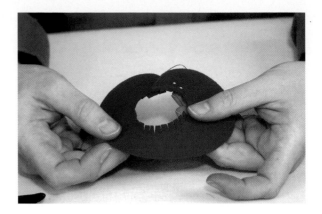

fig.16- Clip head opening approximately 1/4" and fold up collar.

fig.14- Continuation of "Requiem" brim

fig.17- Placing crown over collar

fig.15- Sewing brim together

fig.18- Matching center backs

enough room for the size of the crown and several inches below, which will accommodate the stretching you need to do to have an absolutely smooth crown.

9. *Using a steamer or teakettle give the square a quick steam. Just enough to "loosen" it up and make it a bit more pliable.*

10. *Be careful when steaming anything, especially if you are using a kettle, to keep your fingers and hands from direct contact with the heat. Steam burns are quite awful.*

11. *Center the square on the headblock, and then smooth the fabric so it extends down the sides. Secure the felt to the block with a rubber band or by tying elastic around it. The elastic or rubber band needs to be down far enough on the block to enable you to achieve a smooth line on the felt when you trim it.*

12. *Steam the felt on the block long enough for it to become moist and malleable. Stretch the felt by pulling downward, all around the block. This stretching motion should give you a smooth crown. Keep working the fabric until all the wrinkles are gone.*

13. *Once you are satisfied with your blocking results, let the felt shape dry thoroughly before proceeding to the next step.*

14. *Measure and mark your crown at the desired cut-off point.*

15. *Remove your crown from the block.*

16. *Trim and edge wire the crown, as in chapter 3. For this hat millinery wire was used, shaped into a circle, held together with tie wire and whipstitched to the edge of the brim.*

17. *It is at this point that you could finish off the hat by putting grosgrain on the edge to cover the wire, making sure that it is even on both the inside and outside of the hat and that the inside of the hat looks as neat as possible. Trim it any way you wish with felt flowers as with the sample, feathers, a tiny pin etc. What you then have is a wonderful felt pillbox hat.*

18. *For the Requiem hat we need to take a few extra steps.*

19. *Begin by stitching the brim pieces together. The reason the brim is cut in an open form and stitched together instead of cutting it in one piece is because when you bring the ends together they form a slightly cupped shape.*

20. *The next step is to attach the brim to the crown. With your fingers, press up the notched section of the collar around the head opening. Make sure you're center backs are aligned and insert the collar into the blocked crown.*

21. *The brim is then stab stitched to the collar.*

22. *Once the brim and crown are attached, it is time to put the hatband on.*

fig.25- Inserting stripped feather
through holes

fig.27- Finishing interior of crown
with headband

fig.26- Hat trimmed

fig.28- Possible decorative finish
with scalloping shears

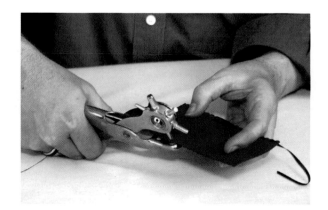

fig.29-Holes punched in scallops
using leather punch

Gene® Marshall, always glamourous, wears a felt pillbox hat, trimmed in "leopard" to match her swing coat perfectly. Repaint by Ken Bartram. "Jaguar" designed by Timothy J. Alberts

67

What could be lovelier than Alex perched delicately on a swing?
"Al Fresco" ensemble designed by Timothy J. Alberts.

Chapter Five- Straw Hats

The story goes, that when they needed a superb straw hat for the barbecue scene in *Gone with the Wind*, David O. Selznick went to Mr. John of John Fredrics in N.Y. and asked him to design and, makc the hat. With the exception of a singular request from Vivien Leigh, that the hat not overwhelm her face, Mr. John was given complete artistic autonomy and allowed to design the hat without interference. The result was a straw leghorn, period perfect, wildly romantic and the ideal frame for Miss Leigh's face. That hat was made using straw braid, one of the two basic options available to you when making a straw hat.

The first process, creating your hat from straw cloth, is much the same as making a felt or buckram one. It involves making a pattern, cutting your pieces from the cloth, and then using a combination of shaping, sewing and steaming to form the hat into the desired style.

The advantage to using straw cloth is that it is quicker to make a hat using it rather than shaping it with straw braid.

Straw cloth is woven with a weft and a warp. Which means it can be blocked. As with other cloths, straw cloth has a straight grain and a bias. In fact the bias on straw cloth has a lot of give, a characteristic that can be a hindrance when making miniature hats. For it means you will have difficulty achieving and maintaining the rounded and curved shapes so essential in any hat and that you'll have to use wire to stabilize the hat, especially on the brims and head openings. And if you wire them, you'll have to camouflage the wire. That is if you can find straw cloth in the first place.

If finding straw cloth eludes you, the fortunate part of making a small hat, is that if you can find a human sized hat, made from a good quality, pliable straw, at a flea market or second hand store, you can cut that down to make your doll's hat. And while you can make an entire hat from straw cloth and that alone, experience has taught us that another effective use of straw cloth in miniature millinery, is to first make a buckram foundation (chapter 3) and then cover it with the straw cloth. The buckram will stabilize the straw cloth, and give it definition and support.

The quality of the straw you use is important whether you use cloth or braid. The finer the straw, the finer the look of the hat. Natural straws are made from a combination of grass and plant fibers, whereas imitation straw is made from synthetic materials, such as cellophane. You can test to see if your straw is imitation by burning the edge. If it beads up, it's imitation.

Both natural and imitation straw will get the job done, but imitation straw is a modern invention and not period appropriate. However, if period accuracy is not of tantamount importance to you, the advantage of using imitation straw is that it steams easily and is very pliable to work with.

Natural straw has to be pliable else it will crack when you are shaping or sewing it. You'll also have to be careful and make sure, when using natural straw that the size and pattern of the weave is of a scale, which suits the size of your doll.

In chapter 2 we use a hat, which has been made from straw cloth as our photo for the chapter heading. You can see how nicely straw cloth lends itself to the making of a hat. This view also gives you an idea of the basic construction involved, something you may find helpful if you choose to use straw cloth.

For our demonstration, in this chapter, we are showing a straw hat made using straw braid. It is much easier to come by these days, and is very versatile, adapting easily to the making of hats of a miniature size. The guidelines for choosing straw braid are the same as for cloth; you need to look for pliability, size of weave, and a scale of braid suitable for the size of your doll.

You'll find that a thinner braid works better for doll hats that a thick or coarse braid, unless you are doing a character doll. Another decision that needs to be made is whether you prefer a braid that has a plain or decorative edge. That is strictly an aesthetic decision, one that will, once again, be influenced by the

Even the most contemporary ladies like to dress up for tea. Robert Tonner's Tyler adds a scarf.
Madame Alexander's Alex's hat is covered in chiffon. Paris wears a hat trimmed with straw lace.
Note the back view of Paris' hat, which is also trimmed with a flower.

outfit the doll is wearing and the occasion it was made for.

To begin, after you have made the design decisions as discussed in chapter 2, you'll need to decide exactly how you want to make the hat. Do you want to sew the braid onto a foundation, shape the braid on a headblock and then sew it together, or do you want to assemble the hat freehand and sew it as you go? Our demonstration hat may help you to decide. For our demonstration we are doing a hat which combines two techniques. The crown will be done on a headblock and the brim will be done freehand using a pattern as a guide.

The hat being made is for a Madame Alexander *Cissy* doll, an 18th century hat, to be worn in the spring.

To begin, because straw has a tendency to crack or break when it is dry, thus making it difficult to circle and sew it, the first step is to soak your straw. Doing so will restore the moisture it lost in the drying process and make the straw more pliable.

Madame Alexander presents "Pompadour Cissy". The hat was made especially for the book by Timothy J. Alberts.

1. *Place the straw in a container that has been filled with warm water, making sure the straw is completely submerged, and let it soak for approx. 5 minutes.*

2. *Remove the straw from the water and roll it in a towel until you are ready to use it. And, if you are working with old or vintage straw, it helps to keep it damp as you are working with it.*

3. *The first thing you do, when making a straw hat, is start with the crown and make what is called a plaque.*

4. *Circling the straw, from the center out, into a rosette shape, makes the plaque, or beginning of a crown.*

5. *Once you have the plaque, place it on your headblock where you can begin to circle the straw, pinning it as you go along.*

6. *This is the same technique you would use if you were making a straw hat on a buckram foundation, only it is somewhat easier making a straw hat on a buckram foundation because you can pin and sew directly into the buckram.*

fig.1- Soaked straw bundle

fig.4- Forming the crown on a block

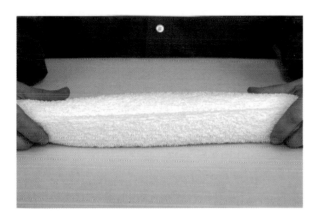

fig.2- Soaked bundle wrapped in towel

fig.5- Forming the crown on a buckram foundation

fig.3- Making the plaque

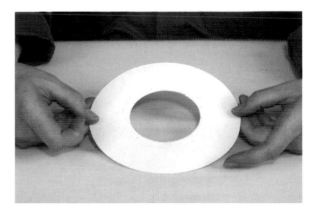

fig.6- Cardstock pattern for brim

7. *The buckram technique aside, straw hats are generally made in the hand and pinned in their entirety or pinned and sewn as you go along. In our opinion, the pin and sew option is the better choice until you have the proper dimension and shape to your crown.*

8. *For the brim you start with a paper pattern.*

9. *Begin by pinning the shape around your pattern, circling, pinning, and stitching as you go along.*

10. *When it comes to sewing your straw hat, you have two options.*

11. *The first is to hand-stitch the brim, loosely, at first and then go over it with the zigzag of a machine.*

12. *With machine sewing, you can either overlap or butt the straw together as you sew.*

13. *The second option is to sew the hat entirely by hand. If this is your choice, take care that no stitches show on the right side of the hat, and that the color thread you use matches the straw.*

14. *When the brim is finished you need to add the collar.*

15. *That is done by adding a circlet of straw inside the finished brim at the head opening. It is this that you will cover with the crown.*

16. *Before the crown goes on you will first need to add a circlet of wire to the brim at the head opening*

17. *The circlet of wire is made by cutting enough millinery wire to accommodate the head opening plus overlap, and forming the wire into a circle using tie wire to make the join. Stitch the circlet in place.*

18. *Now, if you look in the pictures you will see that the brim was made a little short, doesn't reach all the way to the edge of the pattern. The reason for this is because the design calls for a row of decorative straw on the outside edge of the brim.*

19. *The finished hat for* Cissy *is trimmed only with ribbon. We like the classic pairing of ribbon with straw, and think it suits both the hat, the period it is intended for and the doll. But as you know ribbons and bows are not your only options. Flowers and fruit are among other choices available to you for trimming your hat. How about a butterfly?*

20. *Make your trim choice and finish your hat by sewing or gluing (if necessary) your trim in place.*

21. *After you have trimmed your hat, line it and add the headband as demonstrated in chapter 3. Lining a straw hat is a must if you want to protect a hairdo from the roughness of straw.*

Your lovely new hat is now
completely finished.

fig.7- Circling and pinning straw braid on pattern

fig.10- Head wire shaped and joined with tie wire

fig,8- Adding collar to the head opening

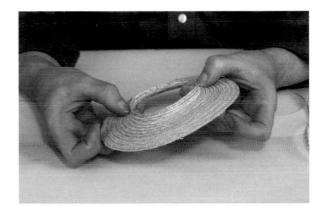

fig.11- Head wire in place ready for stitching

fig.9- Collar stitched in place

fig.12- Area left for adding decorative straw braid

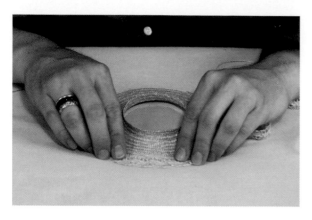

fig.13- Adding decorative straw braid

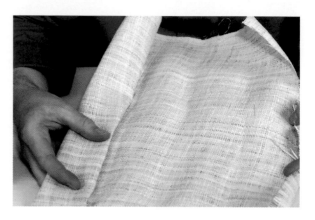

fig.16- A sample of straw cloth

fig.14- Hat with crown attached to brim, and trimmed with ribbon

fig.17- Straw cloth is ideal for covering buckram foudations.

fig.15- Crown lined with a drawstring lining

Overleaf- Madra, Tyler, Alex and Paris are guests of Gene's® for an elegant outdoor tea party. Madra wears "Royal Enclosure", Tyler "Lunch At Two". Paris, Gene and Alex all wear one of a kind designs made for the book.

Cissy Pompadour tours the grounds in her straw hat, perfect for a sunny day.

are not usually interchangeable, which makes it apparent, that each different design, or shape, will require its own customized frame.

The first hat is an Edwardian lace hat made for a duchess; the second a garden party organza made to accessorize an outfit called "Royal Enclosure".

1. To begin make your paper pattern based upon the shape and proportions you desire.

2. Joining three pieces of wire, of the proper length, together, will make the wire frame for the crown and brim.

3. Cut three lengths of wire of the length needed for crown depth and brim width and then allow a little extra. Tie them together, with tie wires, at their center point forming the spokes of a wheel. There will be six spokes.

4. Next, measure out from the center point the depth of your crown, mark the wires and bend them at right angles to the crown.

A garden party hat, made for the costume, "Royal Enclosure", by Timothy J. Alberts

5. Bend your wires, fitting them over your block. Then slip the head wires over them, and tie it in place with tie wire, making sure there is equal distance between the spokes.

6. Make another small circle of wire and place it at the tip, and tie it in place.

7. Measure along the spokes, from the head wire, to determine the depth of the brim. Mark the position on the wires.

8. Bend each of the six spokes up at right angles.

9. Make the edge wire circle to fit inside bent brim wires.

10. Clip the bent tips to ¼", and clamp them down over the brim edge wire.

11. To this you add another brace wire circle between the head wire and the edge wire, and tie in place.

12. At this point you can use watercolors, or fabric pens, to paint and camouflage the wires of the hat.

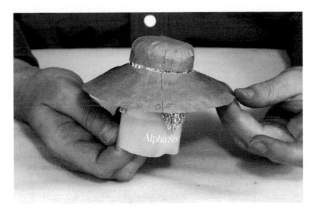

fig.1- Paper pattern used to achieve proper shape and proportion

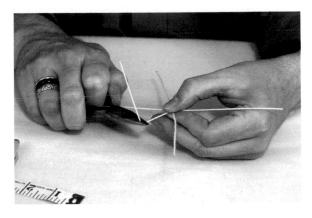

fig.4- Bending wires to form brim spokes

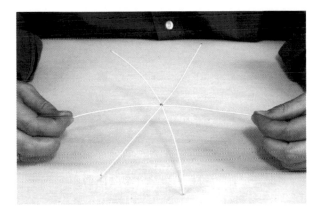

fig.2- Three lengths of millinery wire joined at their center point

fig.5- Crown wires shaped over block

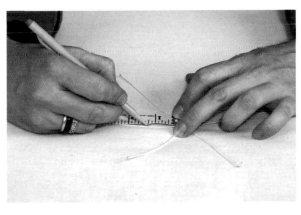

fig.3- Marking depth of crown

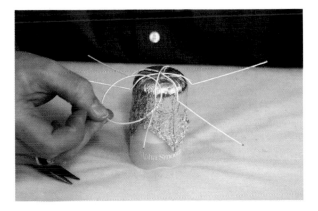

fig.6- Head wire formed to slip over crown wires

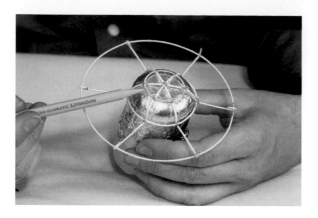

fig.7- Tip wire in place

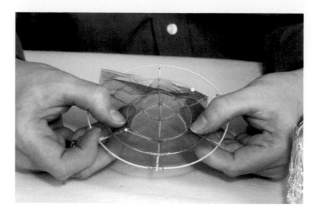

fig.10- Stretching tulle over crown

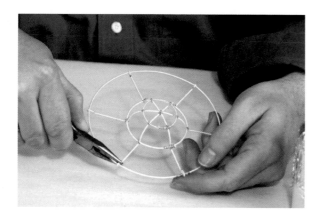

fig.8- Crimping brim wires over
brim edge wire

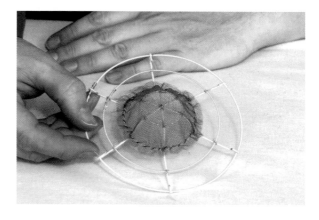

fig.11- Tulle sewn in place

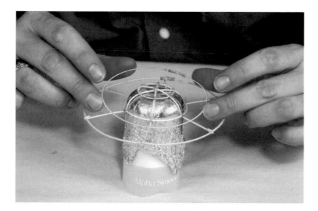

fig.9- Brim wire in place to be tied
with tie wire

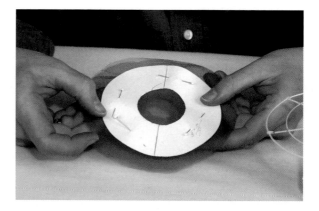

fig.12- Tulle covering for brim, cut
with the aid of a pattern

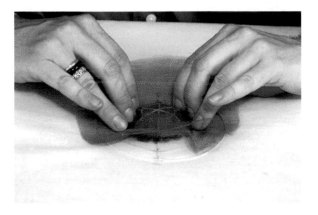

fig.13- Tulle foundation cover placed on upper brim

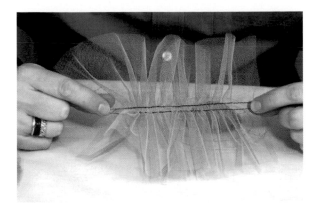

fig.16- Gathering tulle for "French covering"

fig.14- Pinning upper brim cover over edge of brim wire

fig.17- Shirred tulle placed over brim edge wire

fig.15- Under brim tulle covering pinned to the seam allowance of upper brim

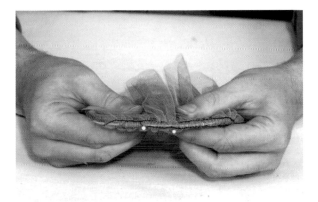

fig.18- Shirred tulle pinned in place on upper and lower brim

fig.19- Finished crown and under
brim

fig.20- Covered outer brim and
crown, with decorative trim applied

13. *Cover the crown with tulle by stretching the fabric over the wires and stitching it in place over the head wire.*

14. *Make a pattern for the brim based upon the wire shape you have made.*

15. *Use your pattern to cut out a couple of layers of tulle, making sure to leave a seam allowance.*

16. *Lay the tulle on top of the brim having notched the head opening to fit over the crown, pin in place.*

17. *Turn seam allowance over the brim and carefully stitch next to the brim edge wire.*

18. *Trim excess seam allowance leaving approximately ¼".*

19. *Stitch the head opening section to the head wire, and neatly trim the clipped seam allowance.*

20. *Repeat this process on the under brim, turning the brim edge allowance in, and then slip stitching it to fabric edge of the upper brim.*

21. *Stitch the head opening allowance to the inside of the crown.*

22. *This layering of tulle is for the foundation only. It is not the cover. It is used to anchor your final covering. It should be as neat and as finished as possible.*

23. *Or, you can use a "French covering", and that is when you used shirred tulle to cover the wires. The tulle is shirred with temporary drawstrings, and the fabric is then carried over the edge of the upper and lower brim, shirred and pinned in place. This will cover both the upper and lower brim.*

24. *The tulle must be caught through both the lower and upper brim, along the brim edge wire, and the secondary brim brace wire, as well as the head wire.*

This transparent hat beautifully complements the sheerness of the dress.
"Royal Enclosure" by Timothy J. Alberts

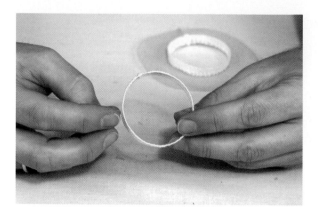

fig.1- Buckram collar with head wire attached

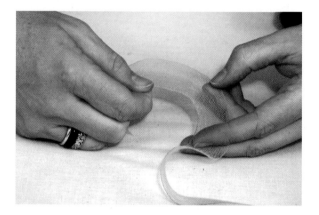

fig.2- Horsehair in drawn into circle with gathering thread

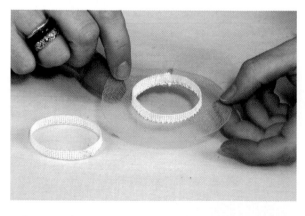

fig.3- Horsehair is attached to collar

fig.4- Horsehair is sandwiched between two layers of organza and caught in place with machine stitching

fig.5- Buckram collar is covered in matching fabric

fig.6- Hat is finished with bias organza ruffles, flowers, and net

25. Remove the temporary drawstrings.

26. The picture of this hat on the opposite page shows the interior of the hat with the French covering, which is used as a final covering for the under brim.

27. You'll also see that once again we've used the drawstring liner for the hat.

28. The finished hat has a covering of lace, a soft draped tulle crown, which has been beaded, a satin hatband, a large satin bow and a rhinestone buckle.

29. Hats such as these really should have the loveliest of hatpins, but beautiful hatpins in dolls size are rarely made and difficult to find. There is a solution, however for dolls who are 16" and taller. Stick pins! There are so many fabulous ones to be found, and they work beautifully with miniature hats.

The Horsehair Hat

1. Begin by making a collar of buckram, which is wired on one edge, the size of your doll's head. The wired edge will be the head wire.

2. Next, attach a horsehair brim to the buckram collar.

3. You do this by shaping the horsehair.

4. To shape the horsehair, take the thread, which is found, at one edge of the horsehair, and pull it, gathering it until you have the size circle you need.

5. Attach the horsehair circle to the collar.

6. The horsehair is sandwiched between two layers of silk organza and the buckram collar is covered in fabric.

7. On top of this can be placed any type of trim you want.

8. Our sample has a silk organza covering of bias ruffles in layers on the top of the brim.

9. The hat is then finished in any way you choose. Our sample is trimmed with silk flowers and a matching color net.

10. A hatband on the inside gives a neat and finished look to the interior of the collar.

Stick pins are the perfect hatpin for the 16" fashion doll.

*Madra makes a regal Grand Duchess. She is wearing a kokochnik,
a traditional headdress worn at the Imperial Russian Court.*

A full length portrait of an Edwardian lady. A one of a kind costume made by Timothy J. Alberts for this book.

Here comes the bride, but wedding bell blues for Liz! Costumes and headdresses by Timothy J. Alberts.

Chapter Seven- Headdresses,
Caps, this & that . . .

The cover shot, *Chloe* with her hair dressed in a classic 1770's hairdo and decorated with that wonderful ship, is not only exquisitely evocative of the time, but is also an excellent example of the very thin line which divides hats and headdresses. This of course begs the question as to what is properly a hat and what is best described as a headdress.

The truth is that, in fact, there is very little difference between the two. Both were very likely created by a milliner or, at the very least, made by employing the techniques discussed and demonstrated in the previous chapters.

Usually when we designate something as a headdress we are referring to very large, elaborate headwear, such as those worn by Las Vegas showgirls or the beauties in the Ziegfeld Follies. Hats seem designated to be more associated with "normal" life. But what is normal? To the nun wearing a wimple, a bishop wearing a mitre, theirs are normal lives. Yet what they wear on their heads is indicative of an unusual role, in life, or otherwise, and their headgear is usually described as a headdress. We have examples of each in this chapter, *Midge* dressed in the simplicity of a nun and *St. Nicholas* wearing an elaborate version of a bishop's mitre.

There was a time when the wearing of the very tall cone shaped headdress known as a hennin, (see visual dictionary) was a common everyday sight. Today it would only be seen in a play or pageant and would now be called a headdress. Which again makes the point that the lines of demarcation between what distinguishes a hat and a headdress are often blurred.

And while most "headdresses" are built from a wire form or foundation, as is so with the grand duchess' Edwardian hat, this needn't always be the case. The ship on the cover, the mitre, and the jeweled kokochnik, worn also by the grand duchess, were all made on a buckram base.

As for the wimple, or "guimple" as it was once known, Webster's defines it thusly, " a covering of silk, linen, or other material

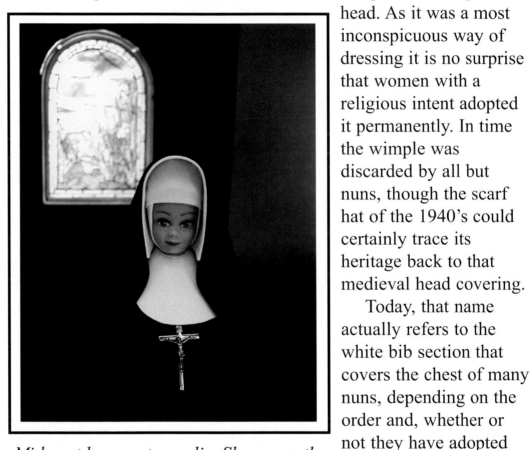

Midge at her most angelic. She wears the traditional habit of the Immaculate Heart of Mary order.

arranged around the head, chin and neck, leaving only the face exposed". Back, several centuries, in medieval times, when women were required to dress for modesty, they covered their heads either by draping fabric in a coif like fashion around their head and face or by cutting a circle and inserting their face through that. An additional piece of fabric, a veil, would often then be pinned on top of the head. As it was a most inconspicuous way of dressing it is no surprise that women with a religious intent adopted it permanently. In time the wimple was discarded by all but nuns, though the scarf hat of the 1940's could certainly trace its heritage back to that medieval head covering.

Today, that name actually refers to the white bib section that covers the chest of many nuns, depending on the order and, whether or not they have adopted modern dress. It is put on over the coif, which is the piece that covers the head, the sides of the face and chin. Finally, there is the collar for around the neck, the headband for the forehead area, the under veil, and the veil itself.

As for the white under veil, it usually is very soft and, as drapeable as the black over

Lace cap on Victorian milliner's model, dormeuse, and cap with lappets, designed by Timothy J. Alberts.

veil. However, there are some orders who heavily starch the under veil, as Tim has done with *Midge*. This starching serves the purpose of supporting the heavy top veil and giving it a distinctive shape. And, there may be yet another reason for starching of the under veil. For the veil restricts a nun's sight, which directs her vision, thus helping her keep her angelic focus.

And while celluloid seems to be slowly taking over, the wimple, coif and, headband if applicable, as well the under veil were traditionally from cotton, as they have been for *Midge*.

Which introduces yet another category, hats or caps that are made completely from fabric and don't rely on a foundation, such as buckram or wire, for their shape. There are several examples in this book; the rose hat *Mary Lou* wears on the back cover, the two cotton hats she wears, the hat *Alex* wears on the beach, and *Gene's* chef hat, not to mention

the three lace caps we also feature. These hats rely on shaped, flat patterned pieces for their construction, many of which you'll find patterns for in the back of this book. Utilizing the patterns along with some basic sewing skills should make it relatively easy to reproduce the hats we show in the photos.

Such is also the case with the lace caps shown here in this chapter. These caps, which can trace their beginnings to the coif and wimple, have been a part of women's wardrobes, depending on prevailing fashion, which dictated the shape of, and how elaborate they would be, right up to the 20th century. Even then they were used as nightcaps by the older generation. The caps shown here are from three different periods, made from fabric only, and do not rely on a foundation for their shape.

The first is a 17th century batiste and lace cap made for *Chloe*, a forerunner of those tall lace headdresses called fontages, so popular

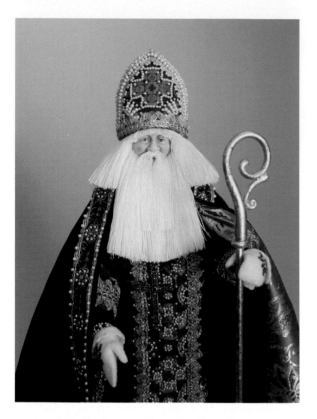

St. Nicholas in his Bishop's mitre.

later in the century. An indicator that a woman was married, the lace cap of the 17th century was worn indoors by itself and under a scarf when the lady went out. Our second example is an 18th century lace cap, again made for *Chloe*. Created from a combination of linen and lace this cap was originally called a "dormeuse", another sign that caps such as these originally served dual roles, as both day and night wear. And as with the 17th century cap, the 18th century cap, as well as the ones from the century that followed, was indicative of a woman's married status in life.

The third lace cap is shown on a French milliner's model. Milliners would often use models like these as a way of keeping ladies up to date on current hat fashions, and, as a means of displaying their skills and artistry to

prospective customers. The model shown here wears a lace cap from the 1840's. Created from a combination of cotton batiste and lace this lovely cap was all the rage with the ladies of that period.

The key to a successful cap is, once you have determined the correct period look, to make sure your pattern pieces and the subsequent fabric shape fits the head as snugly as fashion dictated. For, as with clothes, period heads also had a silhouette and, you'll want to stay true to the correct look in order to give your creation authenticity.

Which means, again, that you'll have research to do. For you'll need to find out if the caps were worn loosely or very tight to the head. And, while you're at it you'll want to check out the look of the trims used at the time you are re-creating. How elaborate were they? Or was classic simplicity, as in the Empire period, the fashion of the day? Was quantities of ribbon looped into rows a desired touch, does the cap tie at the chin rather than hanging loose, or, are you creating a cap from a time when lappets were in vogue? And how long were these long, curved pieces of lace that extended from the side of the head? Should they touch the shoulders or extend as far down as the bosoms?

You shouldn't find it too terribly difficult to makes caps such as these. Using the guidelines for making a pattern, as demonstrated in chapter 3, make the basic cap, using cotton or linen. Then look for lace, in trim shops or flea markets, that most closely approximates the look you need, making sure it is the correct scale. Tack it

Mary Lou at the shore. Costume, doll and hat designed by Timothy J. Alberts.

onto the cap; adding whatever ribbon, or other trim, best suits your design.

And with caps our book comes, nearly, to an end. In the following pages you'll find a visual dictionary, glossary, source guide and patterns, all designed to aid you in adapting the knowledge and techniques we have presented in the previous chapters. But what if your doll needs or wants a hat and you don't have either the time or inclination to make one from scratch? Never fear! There is a solution at hand.

Already available hats! We won't kid you. Finding and buying pre-existing hat bodies for dolls is not easy. It will take a search but they can be found. But an even better bet, especially if you're in a time crunch, is to re-do a hat that came with an outfit or doll.

Straw shapes are the easiest to come by and, depending on how you refurbish them, are versatile canvases upon which you can design any number of different looks. For instance, the straw hat that was re-done for the swing shot was trimmed with a pink gingham ribbon, to match the dress, and flowers. It creates a very young, fresh, and innocent image, whereas the

Alex strolls along on a sunny day in her "Laguna" ensemble and cloth hat.

hat worn by *Alex* at the tea party has been covered with chiffon, tulle and tiny ribbons and presents a much more sophisticated look. The hat that Tyler wears at the tea party is another example. Again, it was a ready made which Tim decorated by tying a chiffon scarf into a bow around the crown. And of course there is the gardening hat *Alex* wears. Ribbon, as well as glued on fruits and vegetables distinguishes it from the others. One style of straw hat given four different looks.

The hat Paris wears at the tea party was also pre-made, the same as the others, but renovated with a slightly different approach. First the hat was dipped in a tea solution to give it a more "natural" straw look. Next a decorative straw braid was sewn around the edge of the hat. Finally, the hat was trimmed with ribbon and flowers, making it a chic accessory for the green dress.

Emily's hat is also one that had been previously made, more demure and simple in its original state, but given a much luxurious look with the addition of curled ostrich feathers and flowers.

Isn't it amazing how the same hat can look so dissimilar when placed on different heads, yet isn't that the way of it when it comes to dolls? Each have their own personality and the same hat, placed on different dolls will give each a look distinctly their own. And that has been one of the messages of this book; hats can play as large a role in defining the character, or life of a doll as the hair, the face paint and perhaps the clothes. Therefore it becomes so very important that the hat suit the doll and, the clothes. That it fits correctly and is in the right scale. But more than anything else it must be "pleasing" to the eye, look exactly right.

In the preceding chapters, we believe, we have given you the tools, the ways and means, to achieve millinery perfection. We wish you success and a miniature cupboard full of lovely little hats.

The basic Emily hat, as seen in Chapter Three, has been trimmed with flowers and curled ostrich feathers.

Lily, a porcelain doll, created by Tim, is dressed as a classic Southern Belle, wearing a hat not unlike that of Scarlett O' Hara.

Chapter Eight- The Hat Dictionary

T he Earliest Hats

Assyrian- In pre-A.D. times one of the first hats worn was a fez type one that the men of the time favored. The difference between this and the one worn by the Turks is that the Assyrian version had no tassel on the top. In the 20th century we have seen the fez on the head of Mussolini and his troops, men who belonged to "lodges", and many who live in Arabic countries such as Egypt.

Palestinian- A precursor to the stocking cap was worn by the early Hebrews around 850-586 B.C.

Byzantine- women were among the first to wear turbans, which are usually associated with the Renaissance. This basic hat shape would grace the heads of women from that time forth, and, make an appearance in one variation or another in practically every civilization or society.

Assyrian   Palestinian   Byzantine   Phyrigian   Scullcap   Coif   Wimple

The Phrygian cap- favored by upper class Anglo-Saxons, evolved over the centuries into the woolen cap worn now in winter by both men and women. What is particularly interesting about this cap is that, even though it has been favored by the nobility, it started out as a cap which was given to Greek and Roman slaves upon freedom, and in later times when noble heads were inclined toward more elegant gear, it spent time as the "must wear" of revolutionaries.

Skullcaps- Worn by the biblical Hebrews for religious purposes, evolved into caps, or as the base for hats, worn by women during various periods such as the 30's and 40's on, and of course one mustn't forget beanies which many a school child has worn at one time or another.

Coif- The "coif" worn from around 1200-1350, would be transformed in the future to baby bonnets, as well as nightcaps, and was the ancestor of many of the tied-under-the chin bonnets women would wear in the centuries that followed.

Wimple- In early gothic times only young virgins (unmarried girls) and Queens were permitted to wear their hair loose and flowing. All other women were required to cover up their hair lest men find it too seductive. Thus the wimple came into being. Later primarily women who took religious orders wore them, but there was a resurgence of the wimple in the 1940's when, combined with a hat it became the height of fashion. Wimples worn by peasant women to protect them from the sun were called "chaperons".

Chaperons were very basic hoods, and as such would travel through history into modern times in a variety of guises. Originally they were worn for a dual purpose, protection from the elements, and modesty. Today, while hoods are still worn for protection, the modesty element has been lost. In fact, wearing a hood can be quite glamorous when it frames a beautiful face.

Caps of all sorts were worn in the 1200's. You can see where many of our modern caps originated, from sport caps to hats with earflaps.

Wide-brimmed hats were popular with travelers and farmers who used them as protection against the elements as far back as the 1100's. Certainly they were popular with the Ancient Greeks, who are said to have worn them first.

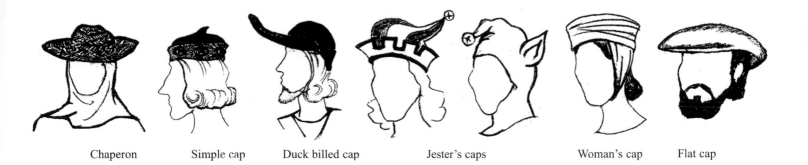

Chaperon   Simple cap   Duck billed cap   Jester's caps   Woman's cap   Flat cap

A woman's cap, which clearly was the inspiration for bellhop hats, as well as hats of the 40's and later the pillbox was popularly worn during gothic times.

The Jester's cap or hat has always been around since they were first introduced in the 1200's.

Brimmed caps or hats were popular during the Renaissance. Available in several different styles, and uniformly low crowned, it is easy to see how the modern fedora got its start.

It was during the Renaissance that the "coif" and the brimless cap combined to become what we now call a scholar's cap.

The hennin, which is a hat that popular culture generally associates with princesses of old, or damsels in distress was admired and worn by French women during the Renaissance. Italian women of the time preferred net caps worn short on the top of their heads or a short cap to which was attached a cascade of net that covered the hair and flowed gracefully down the back.

The kennel headdress (1525-1550) graced the heads of women throughout Europe, though the exact style varied from country to country.

Associated with Mary, Queen of Scots this cap came into vogue in the latter part of the 1500's, and then had a long life as a widow's bonnet for over a hundred years.

From this point on (approx. 1500) many hats, such as caps, turbans & wide brimmed straws, were commonly in use for practical purposes, and would stay so, despite fashion and trends, for the next 500 years.

During Elizabethan times men's caps and hats were adapted for wear by women. Such was the case with a style called the **"sugar loaf"**.

It was during the reign of Charles I (1625-1649) that the beautifully plumed **cavalier hat** epitomized the height of fashion for both men and women. And, while the reign of Charles came to an unfortunate end, the popularity of this hat never did, and in fact, has undergone several incarnations over the centuries.

In a time (1660-1700) when women preferred headdresses of lawn or lace called a **fontage,** the most popular hat of the day was the

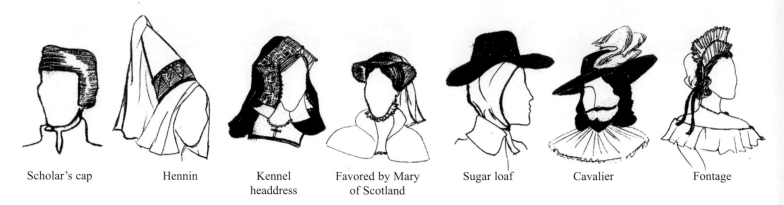

| Scholar's cap | Hennin | Kennel headdress | Favored by Mary of Scotland | Sugar loaf | Cavalier | Fontage |

Quaker hat. And then, when men took this hat and in a spirit of "joie de vivre" folded the brim on three sides, the tricorne was created. Both men and women would wear these hats, the Quaker and the tricorne, for the next 100 years.

The tricorne, Quaker hat, and the wide brimmed straw remained popular throughout the late 18th century. Two additional hats, which gained feminine acclimation, were the **shepherdess hat** and the **calash,** which provided warmth as well as protection from the elements.

The new **turban** was a somewhat more elaborate affair than those worn in earlier times. These sat more on the head rather than enveloping it, and were decorated with feather plumes, lace or ribbon.

The top hat and the **cocked hat** more commonly known as a bicorne, replaced the tricorne for men beginning in the Directoire and continuing through the Empire period (1795-1815). Men such as Washington and Napoleon favored the bicorne, also called the **"chapeau bras"** by the French, because it could be carried easily tucked under an arm.

Hats were extremely popular with women of the Directoire and Empire periods. The mobcap was still sometimes seen but as a larger and frillier version of its previous self, while the smaller version usually found itself perched on the heads of servants and those who were more traditionally minded.

The shepherdess hat and turbans were still to be seen from during the Directoire and Empire.

The **poke bonnet,** available in a myriad of variations became the bonnet of choice for most fashionable ladies of the Empire.

And given the number of battles and wars fought in Europe, during the 20 year span of the Directoire and Empire, principally Waterloo, it is not surprising that a hat for women, modeled on the **military shako,** became vogue, especially when combined with a riding habit.

During the romantic period, 1815-1840, **top hats** were the hat of choice for men. They had been around since 1790 but it took it nearly a quarter of a century for it to become firmly entrenched on men's heads. Even today, while not in common use, the top hat is preferred headwear for formal dress.

Quaker hat   Tricorne   Shepherdess   Turban   Early top hat   A very stylish version of the poke bonnet   Bicorne

Women in the romantic period continued to wear the caps, turbans, Quaker hats, and poke bonnets worn in earlier times, but because fashionable hairdos featured a topknot, which grew in height as the years progressed, the **"leghorn"** was created to accommodate the hairstyle. It was considered a particularly fetching look as it framed the face in an attractive way especially when trimmed with flowers and ribbons or worn over a frilly cap.

Women as well as children of both sexes wore large **toques,** and **berets,** during the romantic era.

For the first part of the Victorian era (1840-1865) when skirts became fuller and eventually led to the use of crinolines, the "leghorn" was still popular but underwent a transformation. Because topknots had been replaced by curls and braids the crown of the hat diminished, as the brim became wider thus framing the face even more.

In the 1850's the **bonnet** became shallower from front to back. These hats were usually decorated with flowers, plumes of feathers, lace and ribbon and held on with, ties. This hat, worn further back on the head, gave the wearer a very attractive, feminine look.

When chignons gained favor in the 1860's, hats started to become smaller and the backs of hats began to disappear altogether.

The **"porkpie",** could also be considered an 1860's forerunner of the 1960's pillbox.

Mr. **Stetson** created his cowboy hat in 1865, and while only those who lived on the plains, in the west and southwest, primarily wore it the popularity of this hat has continued and grown in its universal appeal.

Most men did not wear the Stetson. In fact, most preferred caps, round, felt hats, and the **bowler or Derby** as it was called in the US.

For more formal or serious occasions, the top hat was still a must, especially in Europe.

During the period known as the "bustle", (1865-1890) hat styles changed with great rapidity and frequency. First up were the tiny hats that were made from lace or shirred fabric and worn perched on top of the head. These were not tied on with the lappets of lace and ribbon that often hung down from the hat but rather held in place by wonderful hatpins.

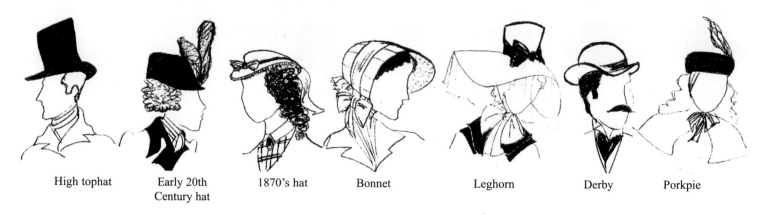

| High tophat | Early 20th Century hat | 1870's hat | Bonnet | Leghorn | Derby | Porkpie |

In the 1870's hats continued to become smaller and to be perched even higher on the slope of the hairdo. And as hats became smaller, face veils changed along with them. Instead of heavier draped veils, lightweight net, often point des prit (or dotted) were pulled down from the hat to just beneath the chin, and secured, by tying or pinning, to the back of the hat.

The late 1870's brought hats that were flatter and wider into fashion. Worn toward the back of the head rather than perched on the forehead this hat eventually evolved into a more modern version of the **poke bonnet**. The more modern version, however, would leave off the ties that held the hat secure, and trust to fate, and the wind that the hat would stay on. Hatpins were sometimes used to take the place of the ties.

From the 1880's up until approx.1895, a variety of hats were popular. Turbans were worn again, the **Tam o' Shanter** was adopted by women and the straw boater became increasingly popular with both sexes.

The 20th Century

The Fin de Siecle or "turn of the century" started out with little **toque** hats, confections of fabric, ribbons, and flowers and net that sat very prettily upon the head. These toques began to increase in size as the 90's progressed toward the end of the century, until the very large hats we associate with the **"Gibson Girl"**, along with the very wide hairdo's that necessitated the need for big hats became the preferred profile for the head.

With women becoming more and more sporty, adaptations of men's hats such as the **fedora** and the **straw boater** were worn with greater frequency.

As the new century began men's hats took on a more modern look with caps fedoras, **slouch hats** and **Panamas** taking the lead. Classics from the previous century such as the top hat and **bowler** would continue to be worn throughout the 20th century.

Women's hats increased in size as the new century began and presented themselves in several variations such as the **motoring hat**,

| Toque | Woman's fedora | Boater | Tam | Gibson Girl | Merry Widow | Stetson |

which always had a protective veil, and the **Merry Widow**. The brims would turn up and down, and the crown, at times, would become absolutely flat, but all these hats, flat crown and all, were beautifully and sumptuously decorated with ribbons, feathers, flowers and even, small birds.

There was a time (1909-1911), a three-year period when the **tricorne** made a return. It served those women who preferred a more tailored looking hat.

In the teens, the shape of hats became higher rather than wider. This change of direction suited the new, smaller hairdos, and the sleeker fashion silhouette.

An interesting look of the late teens and early 20's was the **gaucho hat**. Worn by movie idols such as Valentino and Douglas Fairbanks, this style was adapted mainly by women, and perhaps most interestingly, worn quite often at the beach.

The bell shaped **cloche** was the " it" hat of the 20's. And while the close fit of this hat held fashion in its thrall for most of the 20's, as the decade approached 1927 the brim of the cloche expanded, becoming wider, and would

eventually transform itself into the **garden hat** of the 1930's.

Cole Porter wrote the song "Anything Goes" in the 30's and that was, aside from social commentary, an apt description of the variety of hats popular during that decade. Movies also exerted a great fashion influence on the hats women wore. When Bette Davis sported a **beanie** in *Dark Victory*, more than just college kids wore them. And when Ginger Rogers wore wide brimmed garden hats it was a reflection of what would be seen in fashion magazines. But headwear was not limited to just these two. Women wore small toque-like hats made frothy with tulle, bows, rhinestones, feathers and any enhancement milliners could think of as well as the **Eugenie hat**, turbans and variations of the fedora. The **Tyrolean** hat appeared in 1937 and would be worn in one form or another throughout the rest of the decade.

While going bareheaded was becoming more and more popular, men's hats remained constant up until the 40's when military headgear became fashion statements in and of themselves. **Aviator caps, workman's caps** (worn by both men & women), **sailor hats** and the hat worn by soldiers provided the

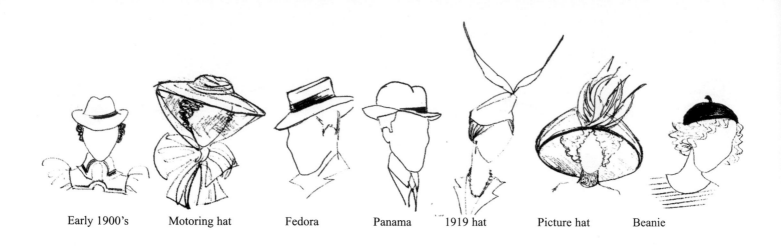

Early 1900's Motoring hat Fedora Panama 1919 hat Picture hat Beanie

profile for the military, while fedoras did duty for those who stayed at home.

Hats were the one area where the women of the 40's could show some flair in their wardrobe. Thanks to designers who created the slim skirt shoulder pad look to accommodate wartime rationing, tall towering hats were created to balance the look. This look also combined hats with scarves and added snoods to the back of hats for a bit of extra verve.

Mannish fedoras were taken the closets of husbands and fathers and combined with suits to create a very professional appearance, as did the Tyrolean hat with its jaunty little feather.

Chic came back in the 50's with Dior's new look and clean, precise lines. Large thin shaped and, wide **picture hats** suited his clothes extremely well. And when you counted in the contributions of Lily Dache, John Fredericks, Sally Victor and all the other talented milliners whose work shone at this time, you could add saucy little **cocktail hats**, large **pancake berets**, and smart turban hats to your wardrobe.

The 1960's were a very mixed bag as far as hats are concerned. On one hand you had the classic look as exemplified by the pillbox worn by Jackie Kennedy and Audrey Hepburn and the oversized fur hat worn by Lara in Dr. Zhivago. Then you had the mod look. **School girl** hats featured by Mary Quant and the big cap look of Rudi Gernreich, or the Beatle cap as it was more commonly known, along with **Juliette caps** and soft, woven full brimmed hats that framed the face are part of the look associated with Carnaby street. But lest the Brits claim all the glory designers such as Halston were expressing themselves with wild and "out-there" hats such as his mirrored hoods. And of course there was the gangster look. Both the **beret** and the **fedora** became hot fashion items with the release of the movie, *"Bonnie & Clyde"*.

The **coolie hat** was certainly a distinct look in the 1960's.

The 70's were, for the most part, the un-hat decade of the 20th century. As hairstyles became bigger and more important hats became less so. Hats were worn to be sure, **peaked baseball caps**, soft felts favored by hippies, **pillboxes** and toques used to emulate ethnic looks. But not until the end of the

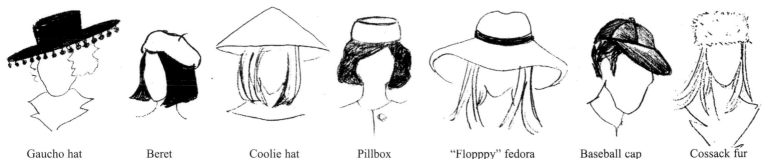

| Gaucho hat | Beret | Coolie hat | Pillbox | "Flopppy" fedora | Baseball cap | Cossack fur hat |

decade did hats make any kind of a definitive statement when the movie *Annie Hall* was released. The **rounded fedora** Diane Keaton wore became an instant fashion hit.

When Princess Diana wore a small felt hat with a feather, ala John Boyd, in the beginning of the 1980's, hats began their return from fashion obscurity. Once again, women wore a variety of styles, big felt and straw hats, small chic hats, the simpler and more school girlish hats favored by the young Diana, turbans, pillboxes, gauchos, the tricorne, and toques. The 80's milliners also distinguished themselves with new and daring looks such as the **"Mad Hatter"** hats so popular for Ascot.

1990's hats were a continuation of what had gone before, in the 80's and, every period where hats had a prominence. As designers went retro and looked for inspiration, hats of the 90's became a glorious mix of past and present. Large hats scrumptiously decorated with feathers and flowers, evocative of the beginning of the century, but looking so very different were created. The pillbox as worn by Diana remained as elegantly chic as ever, and all the other styles captured and re-interpreted by milliners such as Marie Mercie, Jean

Barthet, Patricia Underwood, and Philip Treacy brought a new twist to an old tale.

With the advent of the 21st century hats, both formal and informal, retain a place in our society. Whether worn for fashion or simply for protection from the elements, caps, straws, felts and whatever the new century brings, are clearly here to stay.

Typical of Fifties chic, this whimsical little cocktail hat is made of buckram and net.

Paris and Alex lounging by the pool at Willow House in their hot pink straw hats.

Chapter Nine- Glossary

Beaver: The fur pelts of these animals, along with rabbits, are used to make fur felt, the "queen" of felts. Rarely made, or available in modern times due to a reduction of pelts available, expense, and public distaste regarding fur. Wool and wool/cotton/rayon blends are much less expensive to produce. Beaver was also the nickname used for the expensive and luxurious top hats men wore in the late 18th century and the 19th century. Rabbit, (called coney by the trade), is sometimes used nowadays to make a modern version of this hat but, more often than not these toppers are made from silk.

Brim: The wide part of a hat, which extends outward from the crown, often past the head and creating a frame for the face.

Buckram: A coarse, open weave fabric, usually made from heavily sized cotton, which is used to create foundations for hats.

Cloth wire: This cotton wrapped wire which comes on a small spool is great for use on very small hats in place of the regular (but thicker) millinery wire.

Coif: A head covering, traditionally made from cotton, which served several purposes throughout time starting from the middle ages. Generally combined with a wimple and worn for purposes relating to modesty, the baby bonnet like coif was at one time seen on the heads of most married women. They wore them in the home, under a scarf or hat when they went out, or on their heads when they went to bed. There was such a chaste aspect to coifs, especially when worn with a wimple that female religious orders adopted them as part of their habit.

Crown: The part of the hat that covers the head.

Edge wire: Found on the tip and brim of a hat, the edge wire is sewn to the edge of the tip and brim.

Felt: A non-woven material made from fur, wool, cotton, rayon or a blend of the latter three materials. This fabric, which doesn't have a grain line, and which can be stretched and blocked is ideal for making hats.

Flat Patterning: The process of drafting a pattern rather than draping it.

Foundation: The foundation of a hat is the shape or structure that supports the fabric or whatever materials are being used for a successful completion of a hat design.

Glues: These are used to adhere fabrics to foundations, to glue sections of the hat together, and to attach trims such as feathers and flowers to the hat. (See chapter 2)

Grosgrain ribbon: A ribbed ribbon, usually cotton, rayon, or a blend of both, that is used to finish off the edge of a hat brim, as an interior hatband, or as a sideband on the bottom of a crown of a hat.

Haberdasher: A haberdasher used to primarily be a maker of men's hats, though nowadays a haberdasher sells men's clothes and accessories as well as hats.

Hatband: Located on the exterior of a hat, at the point where the brim meets the crown, (also known as the sideband), the hatband is made from grosgrain or other types of ribbon. Aside from its decorative function, the hatband is used to camouflage the join of the crown to the brim.

Hatter: The maker of men's hats. In times past the term "haberdasher" would also apply.

Headband: Always grosgrain, the headband is located in the interior of a hat, just above the head opening. Its purpose is to absorb sweat.

Headblock: The shape upon which a hat is built. Usually, for humans, it is the exact head size in circumference and can take any shape needed to block a crown. For dolls, you can make your own headblocks using the doll's head as your model, or, you can look around your home for items, which closely approximate the size and shape desired. The hat should be tried on the doll's head from time to time, as you go along, to ensure that it will fit properly and that your scale is correct.

Head Wire: This is the wire, which is placed at the point of connection of the crown to the brim at the head opening.

"Mad as a Hatter": Mercury used to be used for hat making, particularly when dealing with rabbit fur, and the noxious fumes from that element had the unfortunate side effect of causing nerve damage, which had the effect of making the hatters shake wildly. Their quivering appearance was so unusual that those who saw them thought they must be mad, hence the term "Mad as a Hatter".

Milliner: The person who designs and/or makes hats for women. And although there was a time when milliners were women and haberdashers were men, in modern times, both men and women ply the millinery trade, equally. And while millinery is primarily associated with hats, headdresses and specialty headwear is often created by milliners.

Millinery Velvet: This jewel of a fabric is ideal for making hats. Made of either silk or cotton or a combination of both, it's width is only 18". Comparable to velveteen in weight and durability, it has the luster of silk and is the only velvet, apart from upholstery velvet that has pliability and weight without an excess of drape. The backing is firmer so it can be glued if necessary without the glue coming through. Finding this fabric is difficult and our suspicion is it is no longer being made and once old stock runs out it will no longer be obtainable. Should you run across this rarity, buy all you can for it works so beautifully on miniature hats that it would be well worth the cost.

Millinery Wire: A wire, which is covered in either white or black rayon, silk, or cotton and is used to create structures for hats and headdresses. This wire is also used to strengthen brims and the edge of hats, and make them more pliable.

Mohair: Hair of a goat sometimes used, because of it's excellent matting ability, in the making of felt.

Mulling: The process of covering a foundation and/or binding wire edges. Wire edges are bound with a bias strip of muslin or batiste, and foundations are covered with baby flannel.

Needle-board: A rectangular board that looks like a bed of spikes, a needle-board is used to press velvets. Using the board allows you to do so without ruining the nap of the velvet. It is a good practice to press (if necessary), millinery velvet and millinery velour on a needle board.

Needle-nose pliers: Small pliers, which have a long, extended and tapered nose.

Panama: A man's wide brimmed hat which is generally made from a light, fine straw, and had it origins in Panama, hence the name.

Plaque: This is point of origin when making a straw hat. Starting at the center of the tip, you make a small rosette of straw, and then working from the inside out you circle the straw until you have a tip and a crown.

Sideband: The part of the crown, which supports the tip and is attached to the brim.

Silk braid: Strands or ribbons of silk, which are plaited together and then used to make a silk version of a straw hat.

Split straw: This straw, whether braid or cloth, has a very smooth finish.

Tie wire: A very fine wire which is very helpful in the creation of wire foundations, specifically it is used to tie the sections of a wire foundation, where the wires cross, together, thus securing the foundation and making sure your structure doesn't come apart.

Tip: The tip of the hat is just what you might guess it to be, the tip-top section of the hat itself.

Straw braid: Braids made of straw, used in the making of straw hats. Remember the finer the braid the finer the finished hat will look.

Wimple: The combination of a stiff headdress and veil worn by nuns.

The milliner's model, shown full length, wearing her cap with lace lappets.

Always looking chic, Silkstone Barbie® doll models a ready made straw hat, trimmed with ribbon and flowers.

Lina G
All Th
468 M
Morro
805-77
Email:
Metall
ribbon
leaves

M & J
10086
New Y
212-39
Specia
suppli

Mann
26 W.
New
212-8
Mann
such a
lacque
differ
here.

Moku
55 W
New
212-8
Moku
ribbo
organ
assor
and

Chapter Ten- Resources

* All the sources listed here, with the exception of the Doll Artists Workshop, Edinburgh, and Happy Apple Doll Supplies, sell goods which are based on a human sized scale. The trick is to buy as small as you can and adapt the goods to a miniature size.

AA Feather Co.
16 West 36th St.
New York, N.Y. 10018
212-695-9470
This company specializes in natural and dyed feathers as well as silk flowers.

Ben Raymond Co.
545 Broadway
New York, N.Y. 10012
212-966-6966
This company offers lace, trimmings, notions, & flowers for your hats.

Gene® wears "Weekend In Connecticut" while preparing a feast for friends.
Chef's toque and ensemble designed exclusively by Timothy J. Alberts.

Chapter Eleven- Patterns

Pattern making is a highly desirable skill. The techniques involved will serve you in making hats, clothes, or any number of crafts. Knowledge of pattern making, whether it be for flat patterns or ones, which are draped, is not terribly difficult to come by. You can take a class or, you can learn by trial and error. And, quite honestly, even if you are an expert or have taken any number of classes, when it comes to making hats for dolls, there will still be a certain

amount of trial and error involved. You will need, as you draw your pattern pieces, to make sure they will produce the style hat you desire, and that the scale is correct. The best way to accomplish this is, once you have cut your paper pattern pieces out, to tape them together and try the "paper hat" on you doll. If the result is pleasing, take the paper shape apart and use the pieces for your pattern. There is one additional way to learn how to make patterns, and that is to learn by working

Madame Alexander's Alex doll in her "Laguna" hat and outfit, designed by Timothy J. Alberts.

seams. Put the right sides of the hat together and sew around the brim. Pull the hat through the small opening you left in the lining. Hand stitch the opening closed. Press as you go along and when finished, press the brim. Voila, you have a hat. The *Mary Lou* hat is sewn the same exact way.

Note: None of the hat patterns have seam allowances added. Trace the patterns onto the fabric, then cut out the pieces leaving a seam allowance of your choice all the way around. When you pin the pieces together you will have your pencil or mark lines there to use as a guide.

with patterns other people have made. It is for this reason that we supply patterns for some of the hats shown in the book. We think it will give you a leg up to use them as a starting point for your own patterns and hats.

To make *Alex's* cloth hat, cut the pattern pieces out in both fabric and lining, making sure to add a seam allowance all around the pieces. Sew the fabric pieces together; the crown portions first, then sew them to the brim. Then do the same with the lining, leaving a small opening in one of the crown

Mary Lou in the sun. Doll and outfit created by Timothy J. Alberts

PATTERN FOR MARY LOU'S HAT
Seen in This Chapter

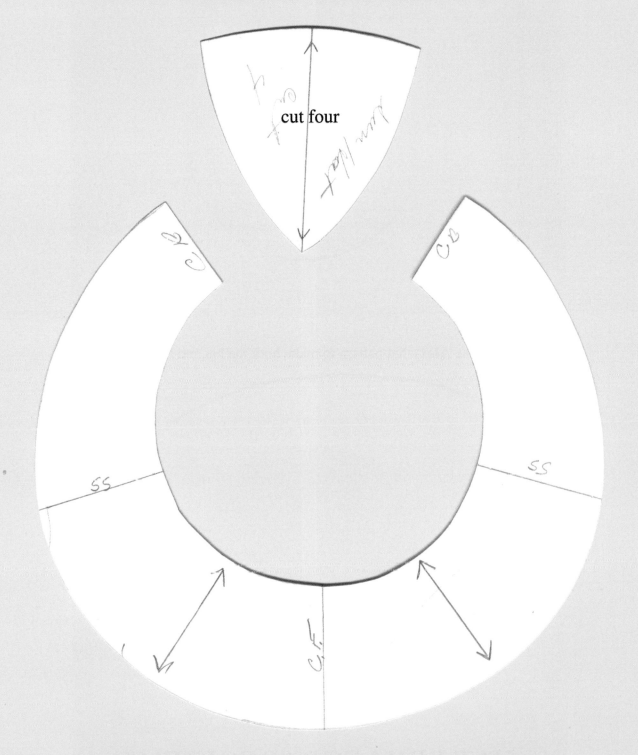

cut four

Use Mary Lou's pattern to make both the hat and lining

HAT PATTERN FOR ALEX'S BEACH HAT

cut four

Use Alex's hat pattern to make both the hat and lining

HAT BRIM FOR "REQUIEM"

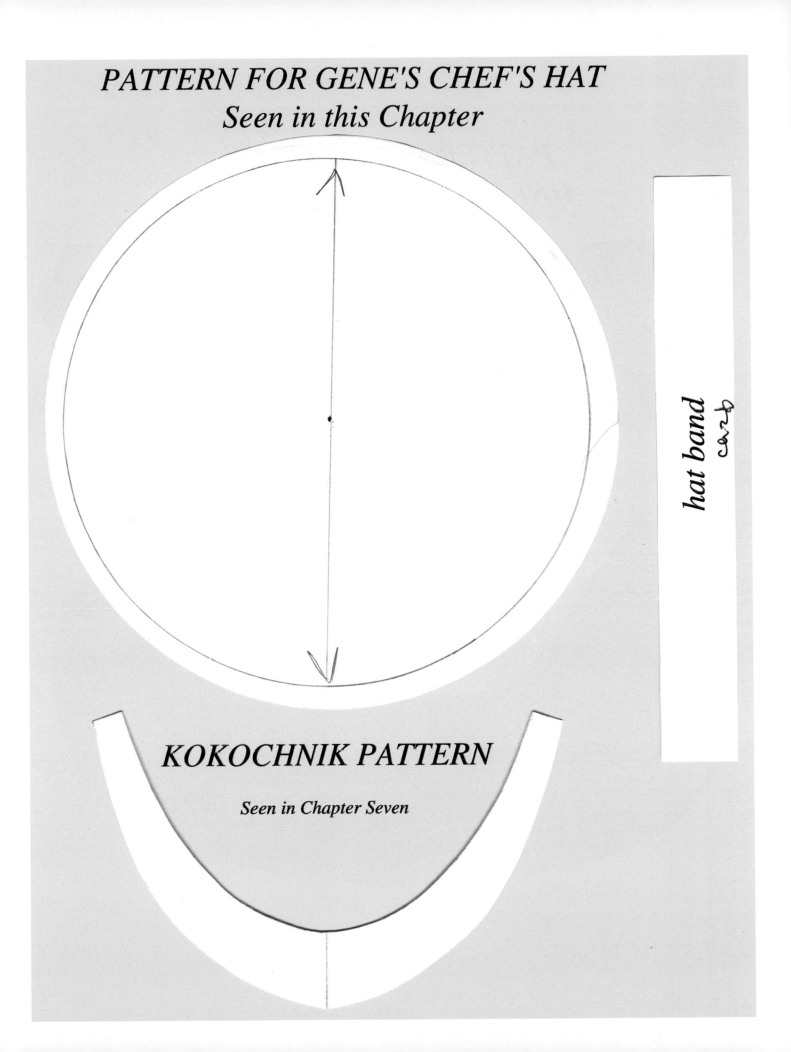

PATTERN FOR GENE'S CHEF'S HAT
Seen in this Chapter

hat band

KOKOCHNIK PATTERN

Seen in Chapter Seven

PATTERN FOR EMILY'S
HAT- *Seen in Chapter Three*

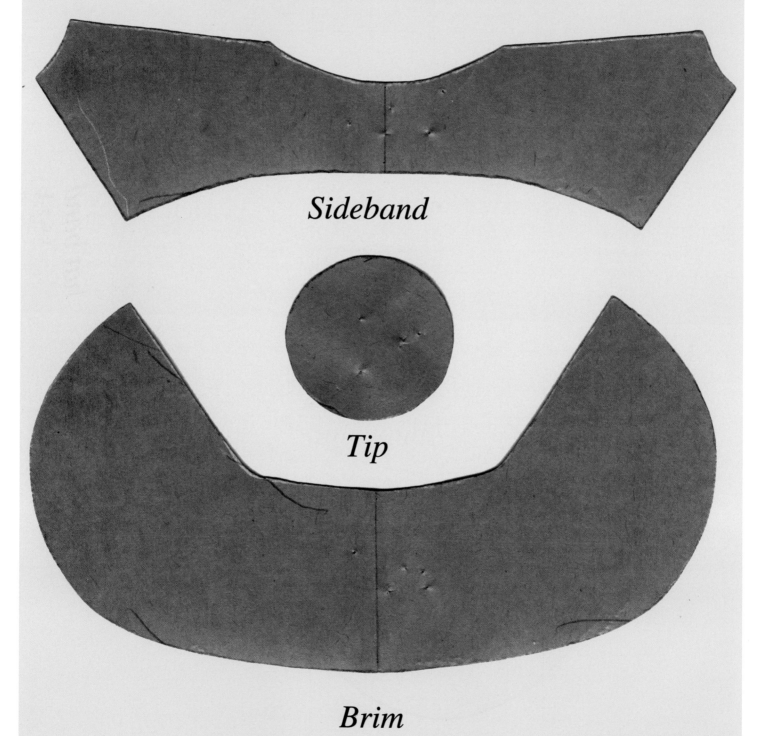

Sideband

Tip

Brim

SIMPLE HAT BOX PATTERN
FOR 16" FASHION DOLLS

*This pattern will make a medium sized hatbox,
or can be used as a large hatbox for
11" fashion dolls*

BOX TOP

INSIDE TOP LID

BOTTOM SIDES

LID BAND

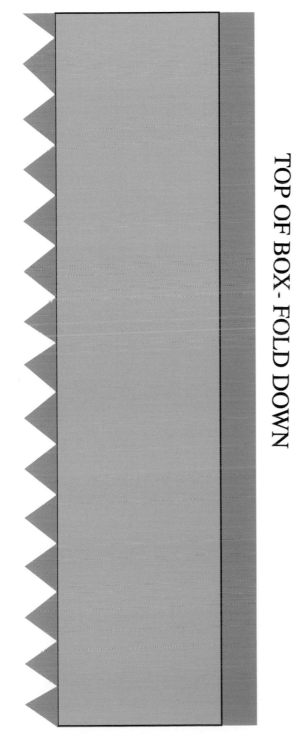

TOP OF BOX - FOLD DOWN

SCORE ALONG MIDDLE LINE

BOX BOTTOM

INSIDE BOTTOM

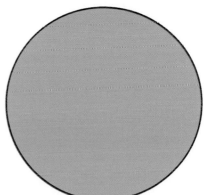

Acknowledgments

Books seldom get done successfully without the generosity of others. Ours is no exception. We have been the beneficiaries of a great deal of help and kindness and for that we would like to thank the following people: Hal Aronow-Theil for his expertise, the use of his studio space as well as his upstate home where we shot the outdoor photos, Rao & Frances Gaddipati for allowing us to shoot on the grounds of their beautiful "Willow House", Wendy Childers for wonderful food and drinks from her "Hollywood Bakery", Ron Tucker for his fabulous outdoor furniture, Patricia Cronin for her Ken Bartram Gene, Isabelle Weill for getting a patio set to us overnight, Marina Royzman for her repaint of the duchess, Sonia Rivera for writing the introduction, and the Alexander Doll Company for arranging to get us one of their lovely Paris dolls.

Finally, huge thanks is due those whose knowledge and information was an immense help to us: Doug James, Lucy Barton—*"Historic Costume for the Stage"*, Jody Shields—*"Hats"*, Denise Dreher—*An "Illustrated Guide to Hatmaking"*, and Colin McDowell—*"Hats"*.

About The Authors

Having gained a great deal of experience from his days at Wayne State University, where he was both a student and assistant designer, Timothy Alberts' first professional job with dolls was to prototype a *Sleeping Beauty* doll for the Franklin Mint. He went on to become known as one of the three original designers for *Gene®*. More recently, he has been working with Madame Alexander on their *Alexandra Fairchild Ford* doll. He has also created four dolls, so far, of his own, which are seen in this book: *Chloe*, *Mary Lou*, and *Rose & Lily*. When not working on films, or designing dolls, Tim works on books such as this one, or it's predecessor, *The Art of Making Beautiful Fashion Doll Shoes*. His work with dolls is prolific, he has in fact created all the clothes and hats featured in this book, designs which will have a public showing in the 2002-2003 season of the Katonah, N.Y. museum.

M Dalton King, the business partner of Timothy Alberts, has been writing professionally for over a decade. Her published credits include, *Special Teas*, *Tea Time*, *Perfect Preserves*, *The Art of Beautiful Fashion Doll Shoes*, and most recently, *Cookies* for Barnes & Noble. She is a member, in good standing, of the Author's Guild.

Pat Henry is a fashion stylist and instructor at New York City's Fashion Institute of Technology. She lives in New York with her husband Hal, and their two fox terriers, Wallis and Edward. In addition to working on the "Alex Project" at MADC, Pat is currently working on her next book, *The Secret Life of Dolls*, and writes for *Barbie Bazaar* and *Dolls In Print*.